Entering the Mind

ENTERING THE MIND

C von Hassett

Waterside Productions

Copyright © 2022 by C von Hassett
www.riotmaterial.com

All rights reserved. This book or any portion thereof may not be reproduced or used in any manner whatsoever without the express written permission of the publisher except for the use of brief quotations in articles and book reviews.

Cover: Consecratory inscriptions on reverse of *Mandala of Manjushri Dharmadhatu Vagishvara*. Tibet, 16th century. Pigments on cloth. Shelly and Donald Rubin Foundation. Courtesy of The Rubin Museum of Art.

First Printing, 2022

ISBN-13: 978-1-956503-83-8 print edition
ISBN-13: 978-1-956503-84-5 ebook edition

Waterside Productions
2055 Oxford Ave
Cardiff, CA 92007
www.waterside.com

To Rachel, my beloved

*With profound gratitude and in loving homage,
I dedicate this book to
The Venerables:*

*Namkhai Norbu Rinpoche
Khenchen Thrangu Rinpoche
Tenzin Wangyal Rinpoche
Tsoknyi Rinpoche
Tulku Urgyen Rinpoche*

Contents

THE PATH 1

The Timeless Pilgrimage and the Pointing Out 3
The Great Perfection 9
The View 13
Toward the Sun 17
Mind 19
Eclipse and Revelation 25
Exiting the Umbra 37
Returning Light 41
The Fourth Time 53

THE PRACTICE 57

Points on Alignment 59
Aids in Our Arrival 63
The Transmission 71
The Natural State 73
Equipoise 79
Ouroboros 85
Objects of Our Gaze 91
The Sound of Wind 95
The I Entity 107
Looking for the Self 113
Ghost Stories 125
Not Finding, Forgiving 129
The Ground 145
Across the Tropics 149
The Journey 157

The Path

The Timeless Pilgrimage and the Pointing Out

Imagine, as an opening tale, you are mid-journey in your travels to meet a great master, a man renowned throughout the world for imparting some of the highest teachings not only on this planet but in the universe entire. This great master, this incomparable sage, has spent his time here on Earth communing with the so-called gods – the supreme source, the enlightened ones, wisdom beings of knowing absolute – and in this transcendent exchange he has spent years and years in quiet, contemplative retreat. Word, however, is fresh-out that he is soon departing, will soon leave his earthly body and move on to higher planes of existence where sentient beings from other lands have requested his timeless instruction. And so it will be.

Before departing, this great master will share a small but essential body of teachings with a select few, conferring his sacred knowledge on those who have shown a willingness to learn, to receive, to grow, to rise above their own limited personhood in an ever-worthy effort to embrace and inhabit their highest and truest selves.

You are one of these most-fortunate individuals. You in all your worthiness have been summoned to meet with this great master, where in recipience of his word you'll at once be one within the lineage of ancient, immortal counsel. Which is why, in this imaginative telling, you are presently on your way to the remote temple where he sits, a sanctum deep in mystic wood where few without high purpose would dare consider venture.

This journey toward the sacred is in the noble tradition of the great pilgrimages of old, when wisdom once was honored and the deeply devout would travel days and even weeks if only to touch the burnished hand of a temple statue. Your journey, however, will not end in the unstirring presence of an idol cast in stone. Rather, you will meet directly with the source, with one who is all-knowing, the wisest of the wise, and you are his way heading to intake his blessings and take into heart the highest, most sacred teachings to be found in any realm – that which will reveal the truth of who you are: the ageless you, the undying you, the you who will continue-on beyond body until time without end.

There is but one thing you must do in gracious return, and that is you must empty yourself totally. You must enter his space as an open vessel, clean of any ideas you have of yourself, of who you currently are, who you've been or what you want to become. You must be totally cleansed – of your beliefs, your history, your wondrous achievements, your perceived faults, your unyielding story . . . all of it, emptied.

And so you set yourself to the practice, to the meditation of release. Here, you quietly sit and little by little let things go. Crossing your legs and resting comfortably upright, you begin to relax and look at your mind. You do nothing more. Just look. What is in there, in this mind-space within? What thoughts? What images? Let whatever you see simply rise and pass on. Follow nothing. Attach to nothing. Merely observe without being led astray. Stay here, right here, remaining observant and aware.

Yet thoughts do rise. Things pull. What is it that calls? What's still in want? What worries lie in restless wait? Whatever it may be, whatever remains, you must, as agreed, let it go. This is the exchange. Simply watch and let all pass.

Continue to look, breathing in through your awareness. What within mind is in need of release? See it and let it go. Breathe it out and be without. Be empty. There must be nothing left. Even the desire for enlightenment must be let go of. Bring in nothing. It is emptiness you seek, an openness of wakeful space and nothing more. Leave all else out: your relationships with friends, with coworkers, your family, your pets, everything you've learned, all your accomplishments, your regrets, your connections to art, to being a spiritual seeker, a good person. None of that will matter in the moment you meet with this great master, so let it go here. You are empty. Totally empty. Are you feeling it? Are you seeing space open in the mind? Spaciousness is what's exclusively sought, and emptiness. Not a nothingness. Not a blankness, but an emptiness that is still aware.

What remains? What is left? What whispers of silent want still ride upon currents of thought? With all that lifts, let them wing into awareness and take to its openness. Do not follow where they go. Do not connect. Merely observe.

Perhaps as you sit an image of your body shapes itself in mind. Observe it and allow it to pass. Do not attach, for it is only an appearance. Even your name, let this too detach from all ideas of who you see yourself to be. Watch the name as you would a withered autumn leaf, and observe its fall as if released from a magnificent old tree. Let all such images, names and attachments, spiral off into the soils of emptiness.

What is still there? You are looking for only emptiness here, and spaciousness, a place of no thing, no thought.

As the emptiness deepens and spaciousness expands, a faint illumination appears of what looks to be the flickering of a lantern. You inhabit no body now, yet you move toward the light upon the radiance of your own awareness. It is effortless, this movement through stillness, and you are completely at ease and at once at the light. You see the sitting sage, this great master your journey was toward, and you see he has been waiting for you and with him you are now one.

Time, he tells you, has passed, and he is on this earth no more. Before him lies the waver of flame from his own finger, and this flame alights a face that too is in waver. His hand extends in an indication to sit and you do, though in this same light you see no body of your own. You are awareness, now, and nothing more, and you are wholly open to his tongueless word.

"Shamans and mystics," he says through the stillness, "call this mind, this awareness you now rest in, an *is-ness*. Some say it is a *such-ness*. It has been called a *that-ness*, while others describe it, simply, as *that which is*.

Look directly at this *is-ness,* this *such-ness*. Do not think about it but only observe. See it. Rest in the emptiness of *that which is* without considering it as such, for in this emptiness that simply is there is nothing to consider, nor is there want for thought. There is only your awareness. You are present in this awareness, yes? And this awareness sees the emptiness of *that which is*, does it not? Awareness sees emptiness, and it sees not two but together they are one, are inseparable. Do you see this?"

Yes, you reply, I think I do.

"In looking at this *is-ness*," he continues, "this emptiness that is at once aware, do you see it as an object or something that can be touched?"

No, you say in the affirmative.

"This *is-ness*," he goes on, "which has no body, no thought, holds no concept of this being this or that being that – does it have a shape or form or a dimension of any kind?

No.

"Yet even without shape or dimension, there is still a knowing, is there not?"

Yes.

"This knowing which is present beyond body or thought, beyond concept or dimension, does it have an origin, an actual point where you see it begins?"

No, I see no beginning.

"Does it have a location?

No.

"Does it go anywhere? In other words, is there a point at which you see it disappear or end?"

It goes nowhere and has no end.

"Does it have an up or down, an inside or out?"

No.

"This *such-ness* you are observing, how close is it to you, or is there any distance between you and it?"

No distance.

"Can it be damaged or destroyed?"

No.

"Can it be labeled, or do you see in it any perceivable identity?"

No, it has no identity.

"Are you creating this knowing, this *is-ness* you are seeing, or does it exist all of its own, without anything creating it?"

It seems nothing is creating it. It's simply there. It exists.

"Can your thinking mind, or that which we call conceptual mind, exist outside or independent of this *is-ness* you are looking at right now?"

No.

"In looking closely at this *is-ness*, which is observed by your awareness, can you say with certainty that it is truly there?"

Yes, it is right there.

"And is it yours? Is this knowing your own?"

Yes.

"This," the great master tells you, "is your own naturally occurring mind, the supreme source of your eternal existence. It is called the natural mind, or mind in its natural state, since like space it naturally *is*. We call it empty mind because it has no beginning and is forever without end. It is absent of any past, and you find no future in it, either. It has no location, shape, or dimension. It cannot be touched, damaged, and will never be destroyed. You can know this mind but not name it, for it is, as said, empty. Yet this emptiness is all-knowing and is eternally aware. All arises in it, including this you see as being yourself. Nothing of you occurs outside of this awareness, and nothing of me now nor ever of anything else. It is always here, this awareness, always with you, and from you it will never depart, not even in your many dyings and the countless rebirths to come, for such comings and goings will not shed from you this one mind which is entirely your own. Come to know this mind. Sit with it, become certain of it, and your search beyond suffering will soon be at end."

With these his last the light went low and the wizened sage went softly to smoke.

The Great Perfection

Dzogchen is like the highest point of a monastery, the golden top-ornament: above it, there is nothing but sky.
—Tulku Urgyen Rinpoche

Dzogchen, or atiyoga, is a profound body of teachings that point us directly toward the recognition of our own mind in its natural state. This state, what in the Tibetan tradition is known as rigpa, is naturally pure and nakedly aware. It is, in other words, awakened, and this already awakened state is present within each of us, is always accessible to us, and through clear instruction it is also easy to identify. In seeing it, we are literally in witness of our own luminous path to liberation, this with one subtle though skillful shift in perspective.

The teachings as a philosophy are radical, if not wholly revolutionary. As a practice, they are transformational, moving one from concept-based being to awareness being, from contrived, dualistic thinking to a mind unbound by mundane thought. This is the wisdom mind, enlightened mind, and our arrival here means there is no turning back. There simply cannot be, for conventional mind has been sliced clean through.

In their sum, the Dzogchen teachings are concise and sword-like, with their single-pointed aim being the direct cutting-through of ordinary conceptual thinking. The direct cut comes the moment we recognize mind's empty essence, and in this recognition we are told to rest and develop realization. In recognizing mind in its natural state, the practitioner is inaugurated into a fundamental shift in perspective, wherein the world is no longer perceived as being *out there,* with an *I* perceiving an *it*. Rather, the new perspective observes all things, all appearances as being *within* the space of one's own dynamic awareness, where it is clearly seen that no 'I' and no 'other' even exist. Emptiness, then, in this ego-collapsing shift of perspective, is not just an abstract concept to be cleverly considered; it is instead an experiential realization, a direct one-to-one knowing of the essential nature of all that arises within the empty, open space of our own boundless awareness.

In Dzogchen meditation we learn to observe the awareness that perceives. We also very loosely observe the myriad objects and appearances that arise in this same awareness, including, most critically, the appearance of ourself – the 'I entity' or ego. Observing our perceived self from the perspective of innate mind is like looking at a scraggly twig or a thin strand of hair held out against the shimmering nightscape of our endlessly expansive universe. It is seen as a mere thing, and a notably negligible one at that.

It is this perspective of self we aim to realize through Dzogchen practice, and it is one in which *Entering the Mind* speaks to through and through: as a philosophy, as a practice, as an awakened state of presence attainable in this one lifetime.

Sacred even today, the Dzogchen teachings until recently were highly secretive and selectively passed along. Rare was a practitioner deemed ready enough to receive such precious treasures from his master, and it was said that even the most advanced students of Dharma might faint upon hearing their whispered transfer. So sacred, in fact, and so secretive, that for centuries in Tibet the teachings were literally transmitted from mouth to ear, and the transmission could only be given once in any master's lifetime. Jean-Luc Achard, in his book *The Six Lamps*, recounts the story of an eighth century Bön master, Gyerpung Nangzher Löpo, who

> handed over the transmission he had received from Tapihritsa to Gyelzik Sechung, when the latter was aged seventy-three. He had previously found out that the best vessel for his transmission

was a three-year-old boy named Mu Tsoge. However, since the child was too young, Gyerpung gave the transmission to Gyelzik Sechung, who was relatively well educated in terms of knowledge and ritual practice. At the time of the transmission, Gyerpung did a retreat lasting five years during which he transmitted the teachings to Gyelzik in a very peculiar way. He had a hole pierced in the wall of his retreat cell and would insert a small straw stalk inside the hole so that the other extremity of the stalk could enter one of Gyelzik's ears. In this way, nobody could hear any word of the transmission. It is reported by later tradition that Gyelzik reached complete realization when he received the transmission and that he attained full Buddhahood within a year. [pp., 5-6]

Even today, elder masters recall a time not so long past when the Dzogchen teachings were imparted directly into the ear via a small, delicate animal horn or bone. This, to the great fortune of us all, is no longer the case. On the contrary, it can be said, in the relative sense, that the instructions are now rather accessible here in the West, and there are a number of truly extraordinary masters currently teaching who are part of a long, unbroken lineage dating back many centuries.

Pointing beyond time or place, beyond matter of any kind, the teachings aim the practitioner toward space itself and to an abiding awareness, our own, which is inseparable from it. It is within this space, that which is empty, where one recognizes mind, that which is aware. This, simply put, cannot be done without instruction, nor can one stabilize in recognition without the continual touchstone of the teachings themselves, coupled with ongoing training, otherwise known as 'the practice.' In recognizing your own mind, you essentially arrive at the starting point, and it is from here where things truly begin to change.

Virtually the entire body of Buddhist teachings, culminating in Dzogchen, are to prepare you for and eventually point you toward the recognition of your own mind. To that end, the several tiers, or vehicles, of

Tibetan Buddhism covey the practitioner from a place of proper conduct to, at the highest level, recognizing the mind. The collective body of Buddhist teachings, then, are progressive, moving the practitioner experientially from 'outward' (behavior/action) to 'inward' (recognition of mind).

In recognizing one's own mind there are really no other teachings, per se; there is only the ongoing practice of continuing to recognize again and again – short moments, repeated many times – until one stabilizes in the recognition of mind, then deepens in the knowing of it. This alone will set the practitioner on the assured path toward awakening.

The View

There is a road leading into the Grand Canyon, Highway 64, that takes you straight into the heart of some of the most magnificent views on the planet. They are literally breathtaking, these views, looking out as they do on both space and split plateaus that plunge deep through the earth and through stratas of time into the Río Colorado below. One could say these views are to die for, for they deliver you headlong into the contemplation of your own imminent death. This contemplation isn't necessarily a philosophical one, though it can certainly be that as well. Rather, it is one which is immediate and visceral and borne entirely of a fall, for you cannot look over the edge of the Grand Canyon without considering your own fall into that great abyss of emptiness. It is this very abyss which gives rise to the canyon's ineffable beauty, as well as highlighting by way of counterpoint the sheer sanctity of the riven land.

This view is much akin to the one we witness of our own mind in its natural state, which too is spacious and even wondrous, a wide-open emptiness that is at once unending and all-encompassing. There is an inexpressible majesty to this view, for it is entirely exalted. The means of transport that leads us to this view is our meditation. Meditation is the vehicle we use to ultimately arrive at our destination. Dzogchen instruction is the road. There is only one destination in meditation, and that is the recognition of the open, expansive nature of our own innate mind – the view. All other roads in meditation are merely sightseeing.

Were you to keep driving once recognizing the overlooks of the Grand Canyon you would be erring on the side of the view, lost in the magnificence of its mind-expanding vistas which lay out endlessly before you. This would be a mistake, and in the Grand Canyon it would be a perilous one. You would be distracted in the state of wonder, wanting to hold onto something that cannot be grasped. The view, then, cannot be continually driven toward, since at some point there is nothing there. The road simply ends.

In the same way, we do not want to be caught up in the view of our meditation, either, attached to its majesty and wide-open wonder, for then we are in yet another state of distraction. Attachment is distraction, and distraction has us right back in conceptual mind. In meditation, once we've arrived at the view we must now leave the vehicle, for it can take us no further. The arrival is the recognition, and when we rest in the view we are no longer meditating, no longer driving, we are merely taking in the mind, deepening in our experience of it and becoming one with it.

The view, being the essence of our own mind, is empty like space yet entirely aware. The awareness is that which sees, wherein space and seeing are inseparably one. It is an omniscient eye, this mind. In it, we rest in the view of emptiness that is simultaneously cognizant, and we become confident in the knowing that the resting *is* the destination. At this point we are no longer meditating and so are no longer in need of the vehicle. Slipping from recognition and becoming distracted means we've wandered from the view, and this warrants the use of the vehicle again, the meditation, where we set out once more to recognize, rest, and stabilize in seeing.

To that end, this book is the map you'll need for navigating the road, and it will take you to the destination just as surely as the map of Arizona takes you to Highway 64, which then leads you straight to the Grand Canyon's life-affirming edge. Here, you are to leave the vehicle at the side of the road, step out and simply enjoy the view, and you do this by doing nothing other than resting in it. Follow the map and you will most certainly arrive at your destination.

The ideas and practices in *Entering the Mind* adhere closely to Dzogchen instruction, while the book elaborates on those profound teachings from the perspective of a longtime practitioner. It can be seen, as said, as a map, or as a manual, of sorts, a step-by-step guidebook for the reader to recognize and ultimately realize their own naturally occurring mind, or what is traditionally called 'mind in its natural state.'

This mind is ever present within us, within each of us. It is also eternally with us and always in wait for our mere recognition, for it is ever-so close. So close is it, in fact, that it is often said our own innate mind is as far from us as our finger is from space. How far must we move a finger to touch space? The mind we aim to recognize is this close, and we must only shift the inner eye just so in order to see it. We make this shift through lucid instruction and regular practice. The instruction is here in *Entering the Mind*, while the practice is your cherished own.

Prior to mind recognition instruction, the other aspect of this book will be to prepare the body for entering the mind, and then help align the intentions of that mind with the higher commitment of a sustainable, lifelong practice. The practice itself, and the ultimate recognition of your own natural state, will inevitably lead to an existence absent of all the anxieties and inherent maladies so many of us face here in the West.

In recognizing this innate mind, then stabilizing in the profound observance of it, what is swiftly removed from our experience is depression, fear, anxiety, anger, aggression, amongst the many other difficulties we dependably experience in our lifetime, and this occurs rather quickly after becoming familiar with the natural state. What's returned is love, joy, compassion, an abiding wisdom and a welcomed sense of near-total ease that pervades each activity we engage in throughout our day, not to mention the beautiful relationships we develop as a result of our own renewed perspective on our lives and the world around us. Indeed, the practices put forth in this book are *that* powerful, in as much as they are thoroughly transformational.

Toward the Sun

You have your awareness, which is stable and unchanging. It cannot be harmed in any way, but more importantly it can never be destroyed. If a meteorite were to streak down from the sky and strike you where you stand, this beyond bad fortune would mean immediate death for the body. Your awareness, however, after a short, restful slumber, would continue-on in a very natural way without the slightest diminishment in its ability to perceive. It would remain stable, cognizant, and ever ongoing. It is this ground-level awareness we call the natural mind, and it is this mind we aim to recognize in our meditation.

We turn away from our natural mind to watch the ceaseless shadow-play of time, much in the way the inhabitants of Plato's cave watched the shadows on the wall and mistook them for real things, real beings. The shadows, however, were rather cast by those outside the cave, backlit by the sun. Turning toward the light at the opening of the cave would have awakened them to the truth, which to this point in their knowing had been deluded by but wraiths on an empty wall. The light of sun in this metaphor is analogous to the luminous rays of our own crystalline awareness, which too casts appearances in all seeming directions and throughout time without end.

We meditate, then, in an effort to fully awaken into the enlightened state, to become the light, and in doing this we come to experience the truly radiant emptiness which allows for all appearances, all existence, to shine wondrously forth. In meditation, we develop a sight that sees this emptiness and simultaneously knows itself, a self-knowing awareness.

Through continued practice we learn to inhabit this all-knowing awareness without being pulled from it by the very shadows this same awareness casts endlessly before us. This would be called enlightened mind were we to inhabit this awakened presence 24 hours a day, even in sleep. Until we've arrived at enlightened mind, we continue to practice, and we do this until we stabilize in both knowing and remaining in our own empty essence, wherein the deluded mind, the one frozen in concepts, awakens into wisdom mind, much in the way a snowflake is absorbed into water and instantly becomes one with the essence of itself.

There are two categories to such so-called shadows arising in mind, one being 'appearances' and the other is 'perceived objects.' Appearances would be thoughts, emotions, feelings, sensations: in other words, all that appears and is experienced internally. Perceived objects are the external appearances of our world which arrive to our minds as form or sound. A black car is a perceived object; the trill of a songbird is a perceived object. Heartbreak is an appearance; the thought of a dog barking is an appearance. All of these are considered empty because when you search through analysis for their actual existence they cannot be found: no car can be found under direct analysis, no song and not a songbird, no heartbreak, no dog nor its bark can be found when one aims the mind's eye at finding their inherent existence. All under analysis can be reduced to absolute zero in form, zero in frequency, and so they are considered empty.

It is this emptiness we must come to realize through meditation, then confidently know, so when things do arise in our awareness we no longer attach, are no longer pulled and thereby distracted. In lieu of the attachment we instead learn to freely allow, just as space allows, and in that single transcendent shift from attachment to allowance all is let be as it simply is. This is nothing short of liberating.

Mind

The word 'mind' is used throughout the Dzogchen teachings in ways that convey the dual meaning of mind being both conceptual *and* nonconceptual, and this can lead to some confusion. The confusion, it should be noted, lies in our own misunderstanding and is in no way the fault of the teachings themselves, for the teachings, after many thousands of years of transmission, are entirely flawless. But to belabor the obvious, conceptual mind sees the world through the subject-object lens, sees an 'I' in relation to 'you,' a 'mine' in relation to 'yours,' a 'this' in relation to 'that.' The nonconceptual mind, on the other hand, is the empty yet cognizant awareness we aim to recognize in our meditation. Both minds have the ability to know, while the latter mind, the nonconceptual one, readily knows itself; the former has yet to arrive at that realization.

The conceptual, dualistic mind has us endlessly distracted in the doing, in striving, craving, hoping, fearing, judging, comparing, even dreaming. It is this dualistic mind that sees, first and foremost, a self in relation to all others. It has a history, a story, a place in which it exists, yet that 'place' is never quite fixed because dualistic mind rarely rests in the present. It also has a quasi-fixed timeline where the self and the story must at some point come to an end, or so it is believed.

This conceptual mind, to leap into metaphor, arises and abides in non-conceptual mind much in the way the smell of gas pervades the emptiness of space. The smell is inseparable from space, which we know to be empty, yet the smell itself is also entirely distinct. You could not isolate one from the other, the smell from the space, even though one does appear to have its own individual qualities. It is in this way that mind abides in mind, the thinking within the innate, and is inseparable from it. Like an odorous gas in the emptiness of space, which eventually dissipates and leaves behind nothing other than naturally empty space, so too will egoic mind cease to operate within innate mind once we come to recognize it, though recognition alone does not equate to awakening. We must also stabilize in that recognition to the point where we realize, where we experientially know.

Why, then, at risk of confusion, do we use the same word 'mind' to refer to both the conceptual mind *and* the non-conceptual mind, the one we set out to recognize through meditation? It is because, in the end, they are no different. One arises in the other, one is the natural expression of the other, one cannot be separated from the other. Mind is like space, with the only difference being mind is aware. Like space, mind is empty, so anything can arise in it, and everything does. Unlike space, mind is aware of these arisals. It sees them. Awareness, however, has the ability to also become duped, to see these arisals as being separate from the space they arise in as well as being distinct from one another, and this is the splitting point between conceptual and nonconceptual mind.

Now, an important point to address is that each mind has its own unique perspective on these arisals, and this unique perspective in the deluded sense gives rise to the self. In perceiving a self, we automatically perceive the other. And though each mind has its own distinct perspective, the awareness giving rise to all perspectives abides nowhere else but in the emptiness of space – the same we see everywhere around us. The space without also seamlessly moves within, and it is through this space in which we perceive. Space also allows for the arisal of thought and appearances in dream.

The perceiver of the dream is not actually physically in the dream, though the dream perspective does not see it this way. While dreaming, the dreamer very much feels embodied in the dream, and that embodied persona responds with either attraction or aversion to all that arises in dream. Dream response tends to feel quite physical, even visceral to the point of being actual, where even the dream body feels arousal, pain, or anything else our in-the-flesh body tends to experience in its waking state. Emotions arise in this same dream body, and we feel sadness, are able to cry, to want, to feel tremendous fear.

Yet upon awakening we see it was only our mind that experienced the appearances of our dream, and these appearances arose exclusively in the space of our own awareness, which is active and ongoing even in sleep. The body we experienced as being solid in the dream, as being vulnerable or sensual, insatiable or imperiled, in fact experienced nothing in that dream since the dream body didn't exist – it was, as is said, empty. Its very arisal in awareness speaks to this emptiness. Look for the dream body in awareness and you'll not find it. Our experience of it only occurs in the emptiness of mind, which self-projects all appearances. This is the essence of emptiness as well as its essential meaning. Emptiness gives rise to appearance, appearance is perceived by awareness, wherein the appearance and the awareness are inseparable from the emptiness. Hence, all is one, or is said to be 'of one taste.'

Moving away from the dream to consider the day, hopefully long off, when we'll experience this same emptiness of our earthly self – our physical body – which in death will be seen as being equally dreamlike: let's then imagine, to extend on the idea above, that you are sitting side-by-side with your best friend or lover. Your bodies are shoulder-to-shoulder, arm-to-arm, and you both feel perfectly relaxed, completely at ease. You both gaze silently and contentedly into the empty space before you, saying nothing. The moment is perfect. Objectively, we are seeing two bodies sitting side by side, and these two bodies have two distinct minds gazing ahead into the emptiness of space.

If, suddenly, both bodies were to instantly vaporize, vanish into thin air, the two minds with their singular perspectives would still remain intact, totally unimpaired, unharmed, still ongoing; each mind-perspective would remain individualized even without their former body to support it.

One mind might likely think, "Oh my, my body has suddenly vanished! Where has it gone?" While the other mind might similarly note, "What the heck!! My body just disappeared. What happened?" Yet the two mind-streams, while still retaining their individual perspectives, would nevertheless be indivisible and indistinguishable from the space they now together inhabit; the space would allow for both minds to inseparably yet individually remain. To an objective observer it would appear as if only the emptiness of space was left. Yet though the space appears empty, the two minds, still abiding in that same space, would remain ever-constant in their own unique perspectives, and onward those perspectives would continue, never to end. In this way we can say "empty like space, yet still aware." Space is the container for our awareness, all awareness, all sentient consciousness, while perspective in the space of awareness remains entirely one's own.

It is for this reason I feel 'mind' is an important word to use when speaking to that which we must recognize, for the word necessarily imparts the connotative sense of it still being individualized, with an awareness that is entirely one's own, as opposed to a word or phrase that connotes something more abstract or generalized.

When, for instance, our own innate, naturally existent mind is instead called 'the Unified Field' – which is how this same space of awareness is described in other traditions – that one shift in referencing can easily lead a practitioner slightly off track, point them just off the mark, since the connotation is now weighted more toward a nothingness or mere emptiness or a field that is somehow unified, a field 'in there' we must somehow transcend into. This, even as metaphor, makes this so-called field less identifiable, and perhaps even unrecognizable to those aiming to see and know *their own* mind. Yet nothing could be further from the truth, nor could it be further afield from our own stellar efforts toward transcending conceptual mind, for in looking inward through Dzogchen practice we see, indeed, that we are able to recognize our own mind in its natural state, and what we see in recognizing this mind is an emptiness that is very much aware, and this awareness we observe as being wholly our own. It is not our neighbor's awareness, nor is it our dog's. And it is not just a mere emptiness, either, because this emptiness is simultaneously cognizant. It knows. More importantly, this knowing has the ability to know itself. Observing this through direct perception is the instance of transcendence.

Eclipse and Revelation

Before entering mind or having any opportunity to recognize its essence, we must first have a body that allows us to freely enter the natural state without awareness itself being impeded by the toxins we take in. The in-flight airplane metaphor is apt: when masks drop in a moment of alert, put yours on first before taking care of others. We must take care of our body first before there is even a chance to remedy the confusion of our own mind. If the body is sick, being poisoned each day by pollutants in our environment, then awareness, too, is hampered by these same toxins. Mind follows body, and when the mind is riddled – be it by thoughts or by the actual poisons absorbed into our flesh – it cannot recognize itself, let alone come to the experiential realization that wisdom-being arrives only from within.

Toxins in our environment are now everywhere around us, yet more critically they are in every meal we ingest, in each vegetable, fruit and packaged snack, and they likewise trace through most of what we drink. What's being sold to us as food in markets and eateries around the world today can be seen as nothing other than a toxin, a pernicious contaminant, an unmitigated poison for the body. This is a point of fact. Agri-giants call these poisons pesticides and herbicides, and they claim that a pesticide used in the field has no harmful effects on the human body. This is an outright falsehood. Make no mistake about it: the poisons that kill both pests and plants in the field do not remain in those fields. The surviving crop, now saturated to its very fiber with the contaminants it's been sprayed with, gets harvested, shipped to market, and once consumed the remnant pesticide gets absorbed directly into the body, wherein bite by bite, meal by meal, year after year, our bodies begin to malfunction, break down, become diseased and move by incremental degrees toward an eventual death.

The advance in years of physiological degeneration has a direct effect on the state of our minds, making it difficult to focus, formulate thought, form healthy intentions and habits, let alone productively function on a day-to-day basis. As it pertains to the transformative practice of realizing the essence of innate mind: if our brains are in an interminable fog, then what are the chances of looking through that fog to see mind's inherent nature? They are not good. It is best, then, if you are seeking to elevate your heart and mind, to make it your sole focus to return well-being into the body, to bring it back into a state of optimal health. Only in doing this will you be able to achieve your higher purpose, whatever that purpose may be.

If your aim is to recognize your own wisdom mind, then you must cleanse yourself of the poisons you take in through diet. The most important change you can make in doing this is to eat and drink exclusively organic foods, preferably locally farmed or home grown. And while organic isn't perfect, it is good enough to save your life and is far superior to the industrial feed which currently is our only grocer alternative.

The handful of conglomerates now producing the world's foods control virtually the entire system of production as well, from seed to supermarket shelves. These goliath companies are earth-altering entities unto themselves, all powerful and all controlling, world dominant and dominating beyond what's good for the earth or wholesome for her inhabitants. As hulking giants in industries managing the global production of what we eat, they remain heedless to the noisome peripherals of their trade, their partners, the markets they control or the soils they exploit. They care little, for instance, about the lives of the farmers they do business with, and they care even less about the health and wellbeing of those they are claiming to feed. They similarly have little regard and shirk all responsibility for the land they mindlessly strip, the soils they ravage and the waters they poison beyond any compunction. In other words, wherever these companies stake both their logos and their claim, the surrounding terrain is put on fast track toward total ruin.

For each of these companies, the purpose behind their enormous profits is to produce or deliver 'product,' and their single-minded objective is to get that product to market as swiftly, cheaply, and systematically as possible. Not one of these companies see their product for what it should actually be – food – for if they did, their methods of production would come quickly into alignment with the basic demands of both the earth and the human body, and what that body fundamentally needs to both survive and thrive.

Instead, what arrives on our supermarket shelves not only directly counters our thriving, it is now imperiling our very ability to survive, and I'm not just speaking about us as individuals but us as a collective humanity. All evidence is pointing toward the collapse of our kind, as well as every other living species on the planet, and this collapse is imminent – in a matter of decades. A key cause for this collapse is the methods of production of our food, which on its own is killing much of what lives on the planet, including its soils, its water systems, the diversity of plants and the kingdom of animals once nourished by the land. All the while, the quality of the food arriving in our markets is literally laying waste to the human body. And so a collapse is at hand.

But I misspeak in calling this product 'food,' since the vast majority of comestibles in our markets today cannot by any standard be considered food, or at least what our relatives and ancestors only a few decades ago might have called food. 'Industrial feed' might be the better term, for the food-like product we now find in markets around the world has long strayed, nutritionally speaking, from the template of the original. I'll altogether bypass the discussion of processed food, since it is universally agreed that these shelf products belie the very category of food, being they are more concoctions of chemistries for the slavering palate, requisite in calories and little else. I'll likewise judiciously avoid any discussion of the wholesale atrocities and veritable horrors seen as general practices in meat industries across the planet. Yes, we can agree that meat products are food in the traditional sense, but the manner in which the bloodless apparatus churns out this living product, good conscience alone should have you avoiding any intake of this chemical-infused, hormone-fattened, cancer-ridden, fear-saturated substance that is so wholesomely sold to us as "fresh, farm-raised meat for your family's healthful consumption."

Rather, I'll speak only to what can generally be agreed upon as being 'real' food in today's market: that of the humble plant. Who could deny that kale or broccoli, a carrot or green bean, a tomato or sweet, crispy apple is not food? By all appearances they most certainly are. Indeed, these products have never been prettier or more pristine looking than they show themselves to be in our markets today. They truly are a wonder, immaculate simulations of what their historical kin once looked like in the wild. Yet leave it to the agri-giants to turn the once beloved plant into an alien other. A head of kale, for instance, certainly *looks like* kale, a green bean *looks like* a green bean, but what you are ingesting is entirely something else, and far more harmful to your health.

Turning a hard gaze on but one of the corporate giants, who for years held heavy sway over vast swaths of agribusiness – the long-maligned, now slumbered Monsanto[1] – we can begin to get our heads around the sheer breadth of planetary carnage resulting from just one of their products, glyphosate, which is literally bringing the full spectrum of living systems on Earth to the brink of total collapse. Glyphosate, once known in a slightly different formulation as Agent Orange, and currently marketed to consumers under the name Roundup®, is perhaps the greatest threat not just to humanity but to all life on this earth, bar none.

Glyphosate is both herbicide and antibiotic, and it is being dumped into the soils and water systems across the globe at a rate of about 4.5 billion pounds per year. The substance is water soluble, so once sprayed on

---

[1] Monsanto has since been acquired by Bayer, who promptly discontinued the Monsanto name but still manages its array of products, which are now a part of Bayer's 'healthy portfolio.'

crops it floods off our fields into nearby streams, lakes and river systems across the land, poisoning the waters and killing most of its plant-life as it washes perilously downward toward our oceans, which themselves have become dead zones in the unabating runoff.

Not only is glyphosate approved by governments around the world – with the United States taking the lead in sanctioning and subsidizing the ruinous practice – its use on American farms was, prior to the company being purchased by Bayer, unconditionally mandated by Monsanto, who then sold these same farmers the genetically modified seeds which could survive the herbicide's ravaging effects. But not just the soils are ravaged by glyphosate, and not just non-genetically modified plants: the human body, as well, is slowly laid to ruin by this deadly poison.

There are 20+ amino acids needed to build protein and thus maintain a healthy human body. Nine of those amino acids cannot be made by the body, so they must be taken-in through food. These nine aminos are known as 'essential,' and they are produced in our environment by bacteria, fungi, and plants. Certain plants have become staple crops – corn, wheat, soybeans, are all staples. Farmers, at the none-too-subtle directive of the chemical giants who sell them the seed, the spray, the equipment used to harvest, are 'encouraged' to plant only one crop in their fields, and this becomes their staple crop. All other plants in the field, now perceived as being weeds, must be eradicated. Glyphosate is sprayed on the fields to do just that. The chemical would surely kill the crop as well were it not for the genetically engineered seeds these same chemical giants produce to survive their own pesticides. So now all but the seeding crop dies in the field, or that's ideally how it's supposed to work.

But more than killing all naturally occurring, non-genetically engineered plant life on top of the soil, glyphosate also kills the bacteria and fungi beneath the soils, along with the parasites and other micro-organisms that together make our soils rich and sustainable for growth of any kind to occur at the surface. This truly magnificent ecosystem living beneath the soil also creates an essential communication network for all life within and above the soil to tap into, and all life connected to those soils use that network for a balanced and thriving existence throughout.

Glyphosate shuts down that entire network by effectively sterilizing the soil, which is another way of saying it kills virtually everything alive beneath the soil's surface. This is all considered collateral damage, of course – not the intended effect – since its primary targets are the plants above the soil, and it is an assassin of the highest order in getting that job done. The herbicide, however, kills pretty much all organic matter existing both above and below the topsoil.

Glyphosate kills by targeting the shikimate pathway in plants, bacteria and fungi. The shikimate pathway allows these organisms to synthesize the very compounds they need for survival. Key amongst those compounds are three of the nine amino acids our bodies need to build protein: tryptophan, which makes serotonin in our bodies, phenylalanine and tyrosine, which produce dopamine. Naturally occurring glycine, which is one of the nine essential amino acids and is also the backbone of glyphosate (N-phosphonomethyl glycine), is appropriated and essentially replaced in the body by the lab-concocted, non-coding, non-deployable version found in glyphosate. As a result, the body can no longer functionally utilize that amino acid as well, so now there are four out of nine *essential* amino acids either removed or rendered non-functional in our bodies with the ingestion of just one chemical used in our farming practices. There are many dozens, if not hundreds of these kinds of chemicals sprayed on farmlands throughout the world, each and every one of them meant to kill something, and all of them will have adverse effects on both our bodies and our minds. In this discussion, however, we will keep our focus only on the one chemical, glyphosate, to see the radical and utterly catastrophic effects this one substance has on the human body.

To survive glyphosate a plant must be genetically modified, hence the acronym GMO, for Genetically Modified Organism. A seed is modified in the lab to essentially bypass any dependency on the compounds traditionally synthesized in the shikimate pathway, and so no longer does the plant need, nor will it contain, three of the essential amino acids our bodies require. With one chemical, and with one genetic modification intended to subvert nature's propensity for diversity, we lose a critical one-third of the essential amino acids our brains need to remain functional. So while the plant, say a head of broccoli, most certainly looks like the broccoli nature intended it to be – its appearance puts forward the impression that it is healthy for us – it is now devoid of the very essentials we'd expect it to have and are looking to take in when eating it. It still offers the fiber, but what's needed for the brain to properly function is no longer there, for it was genetically excised from the seed.

Think of those nine amino acids as vowels. If you remove one vowel from the language you still have a functioning language, albeit notably hobbled. Remove nearly half of all vowels and a language will assuredly collapse. It will become nonfunctional, and the resultant expression will be gibberish. This is what happens to the chemical balance of our brains when taking in a totality of foods engineered to withstand glyphosate. The brain begins to malfunction, and we sense an ominous wintering of the mind, an erasure of mental clarity that is euphemistically referred to as 'brain fog.' This is the front end of the glyphosate cycle, or what we might equate to the topsoil effect.

Glyphosate arrives in the body with each non-organically produced vegetable we buy and ingest, and once consumed the herbicide disrupts the body's myriad complex systems much as it disrupts the enzyme pathways in all non-genetically modified organisms it comes in contact with in the soil – before actually killing those otherwise healthy organisms where they lay.

So how does glyphosate impair us as individuals and imperil us collectively as a species? When glyphosate enters the body through food and drink, it immediately begins to kill-off the body's microbiome, which is equatively the same microbiome found in the earth's soils. Soils, if you recall, are teeming with fungi, bacteria, viruses and parasites, and it is this vast living network that allows for the plant kingdom above the soils to thrive. Our bodies are similarly teeming with fungi, bacteria, viruses and parasites, all working together in natural alliance to help regulate the human organism so that all systems function normally. When the soils of our body begin to fail, the organism on the whole begins to fail.

The human body contains roughly 100 trillion cells. Living in magnificent harmony with those 100 trillion cells are the 'non-human' organisms native to the body's diverse microbiome. There is something like two quadrillion bacteria living in the healthy human body, of which there are roughly 30 to 40 thousand species of bacteria alone. There are an estimated 300,000 different species of parasites living in the body, the majority of which help regulate healthy cell function. There are a million species of fungi living in a healthy microbiome, a number that might seem slight when compared to the estimated 380 trillion viruses teeming throughout the body. That number, again, is a mere pittance in comparison to the actual number of viruses in existence on the planet, which is a jaw-dropping 10 to the 31 in number – that's 10 with 31 zeros after it, or ten nonillion – a number, by the way, that is greater than the number of stars in the vast sweep of our universe. These are the organisms and genetic material that make up a *healthy* human microbiome.

The function of the microbiome is to help regulate the entire ecosystem of our body. It not only keeps us healthy, it keeps us alive. We spoke of 100 trillion cells in the human body. In each and every one of those cells there are an estimated 36 billion chemical changes taking place every second. Multiply those 36 billion changes by 100 trillion cells and, well, you have a grand symphony of change taking place in the body every second you are alive. It is the function of the microbiome to help all those incredibly numerous changes happen normally, efficiently, and in perpetuity for the entire course of our life on this planet. To that end, for most of humanity's time here on Earth, the microbiome has done a remarkable job of evolving with the very planet it is in existence with, keeping our bodies one-to-one with an ever-changing environment that, were it not for the microbiome, we as a species would have died off a long time ago.

Then comes glyphosate. Glyphosate attacks the microbiome immediately upon entry, and in the short run it wholly compromises it before it ultimately exterminates it. With the intake of glyphosate through our foods, the herbicide does within us exactly what it does to lifeforms and ecosystems without: it kills fungi, bacteria, viruses and parasites. Its stated purpose is to kill exclusively insects and plants, but the knowing consequence of this usage by all who promote it and deploy it in the field is the wholesale ruin of our soils and the outright destruction of all life within those soils. Also known by all who promote it and those who deploy it in the fields is that glyphosate once sprayed in the fields does not remain in those fields. From topsoil to subsoil and into the water and weather systems now circling the globe, glyphosate is wholly amongst us. It is in the water we drink and the air we breathe, and were we to stop using this one chemical today it would still take another half-century for it to notably diminish from the environment.

Glyphosate was first officially approved for use on crops in the United States in 1992, when it was initially sprayed on wheat crops. What swiftly followed, a historical anomaly, was a sudden spike in wheat allergies and an alarming, equally sudden intolerance of gluten appearing throughout the US around this time. This raised no red flags with the US regulating agencies whose job it was to protect an unwitting populous. They should have, per their mission, put an immediate end to the spraying of glyphosate on all US crops. Instead, by 1996 the greenlight was officially given to spray the lethal herbicide on all staple crops. What ensued can now be viewed as an outright humanitarian disaster.

In the decades prior to the 1990s, statistics showed a very stable rate of autism in children across the United States. Autism is a brain *injury* that takes place in children typically between 18 months and two years of age. Autism rates in the US pre-1990s were steady at roughly 1 in 5000 children, and that ratio had remained relatively unchanged for many decades prior. Throughout the 1990s, however, the rate began to swiftly tick upwards. Today, the rate of autism in this same age group is

1 in 40 children, where it continues to steadily rise. From 1 in 5000 to 1 in 40 in a mere 30 years!

At the other end of the generation timeline we are witnessing similarly proliferating rates of Parkinson's in elderly men and Alzheimer's in elderly women. Sleep and depression disorders are now rampant throughout the population, far beyond what was seen before the turn of this century. Whereas 1 in 100 individuals experienced depression at the turn of the 20th century, the calculus is now 1 in 2 individuals suffering from some form of depression. 1 in 10 children are now diagnosed with having attention deficit disorder (ADD), and 1 in 7 of those children are now medicated for the syndrome. 1 in 4 children, or 25%, now have asthma, a percentage that is well up from the 4% of children having asthma prior to the widespread use of glyphosate. The same ratio, 1 in 4, is the new rate of occurrence for children with food allergies, and food allergies throughout the population has risen dramatically in recent decades.

Cancer rates have exploded since the introduction of glyphosate into our food systems, and cancers that were once exclusively found in the elderly are now becoming all-too common in children – bone marrow cancers and brain tumors in particular. Since the introduction of glyphosate, and a direct result of its usage, we now have a region in the US called Cancer Alley. Located in the last 90 miles of the Mississippi River, this area of the Midwest is where glyphosate pours off surrounding farmlands into the mighty river and its incoming tributaries. Those last 90 miles, between Baton Rouge and New Orleans, now has the highest rate of cancer in the entire developed world, a rate that is *50 times higher* than the national average.

American men have seen a 50% decline in their sperm count in the last two decades alone, while 1 in 3 men now have a sperm count so low that they will not be able to have children.

Chronic fatigue comes as the direct result of our intake of pesticides through food. If you are feeling endlessly tired, endlessly without the energy you need to get through the day, it is likely you are suffering from the debilitating effects of glyphosate – which even if your food is being sprayed with a pesticide using a different name, the key ingredient will likely be glyphosate. Fatigue in the chronic sense is symptomatic, a signifier of something dangerously wrong in the overall functioning of your body, and it is telling you the time is now to make an immediate change. That change can only be the full removal of all foods sprayed with pesticides.

I'll speak briefly to personal experience on this, since I too went through a prolonged period, several years, of experiencing the kind of exhaustion that felt alien to my body, as if a foreign entity had stolen in and taken over. Little did I know how true that was. The feeling was insidious and was present without relent. At the time I wasn't buying organic, but I was mostly vegetarian and fully believed my diet was excellent. Nevertheless, I felt the interminable malaise of fatigue that was mixed in with occasional days of feeling not just tired, but sickly. I couldn't get my head around it, and the more careful and selective I became with the food I was putting into my body – doing everything in my power to regain energy, to clear away the mental haze – the symptoms remained maddeningly constant.

At some point through research I came across the glyphosate connection, and shortly after I decided to experiment with buying exclusively organic. Those first few weeks I put nothing in my body that wasn't organic. Every vegetable was organic, dairy was organic, even coffee went organic. Within a week I felt my body begin to change, as if it were *recombining* – a strange word to use, I know, but it turns out the sensation was appropriate to what was actually happening internally. Things were literally coming back together on the inside. I was still tired those first few weeks, but it was a different kind of tiredness, a cleaner one. Within a month, and for the first time in several years, I began to feel good again. My head had cleared. My body felt clean and *intact*. It turns out glyphosate causes the inner landscape of the body to come undone in the actual sense. You hear phrases like 'leaky gut.' This is literal. The tight junctions that line the entire gut begin to break apart and seepage occurs. The blood-brain barrier breaks down, and toxins from the body begin to infiltrate the brain. This leads to brain fog and other mental and emotional conditions. Organs lose their capacity to cleanse, to flush the body clean, and so toxins build within the body and all subtle maladies move toward the chronic.

We cannot talk about finding our higher selves, or recognizing the nature of our innate minds, when the body itself is hemorrhaging from within. With the intake of glyphosate through nearly every non-organic food and drink, the body finds itself falling more and more sickly, and little by little the escalating signs of system failure come into full reveal. Mind follows body, so if the body is healthy then mind has the ability to elevate, to awaken into its natural state. It cannot do this if the body is being poisoned with every meal, with each daily snack, with the sip of our every drink.

The takeaway here is to put your hard-earned cash toward the more conscious and noble cause of not only healing your own good self but the planet as well. This means buying exclusively organic. Buy organic and you'll be supporting farmers who choose, at great risk to their livelihoods, to defy the corporate establishment now controlling all aspects of agribusiness. Buy only organic and your dollars go toward healing the planet, in that the planet is similarly suffering as a direct result of our use of injurious chemicals.

Your body is the soil within which your thinking mind is rooted. If that soil is poisoned, laid barren, then the mind cannot find its way to the light. If your goal is to enlighten, to realize the magnificence of your own natural state, then it is essential that you nurture, like a mother would her child, the very body that supports the mind you aim to uplift.

Exiting the Umbra

The wholesale intake of pesticides most certainly challenges the body, imbalances it, weakens it, wherein the long, slow arc of deterioration begins. As the body fights to maintain some semblance of health, then fights to fend off the assailants of that health, then cuts its losses when something can't be saved – an organ here, a leg there – until at last the fight is given up altogether, the mind through all of these small losses retreats little by little from the substance of ourselves, our actual flesh, and withdraws further and further from the frontline warfare now wreaking havoc on the very cells of our being. Know that the losses do not need to be large for the mind to retreat from the body. As cells die off, the mind pulls straight out of these onetime micro-containers in the same way it withdraws from the body upon death. Mind inhabits our cells to the total of ourselves, and one by one as cells die from pesticides, the mind, one cell at a time, bids us adieu.

To use another imperfect analogy, the mind backs further and further away from the home it lives in because the home itself is a house on fire. If your own home were to catch fire and you had the option of sticking around to save it, you first would retreat to rooms away from the flames or smartly head to areas where you could at least be safe. The mind does something like this when the body becomes too inflamed – an early indication that the body's first lines of defense have been breached. The mind moves still further from areas within the body that are beginning to outright fail, which is when pesticide saturation becomes chronic. Its last, worst option is to flee the body altogether, and this means the house burns down, collapses forthright. Death certificates tend to read: patient died from organ failure, stroke, cancer, brain degeneration. But be assured that the primary cause of all the modern-day maladies which ultimately slay us are the poisons we take in through our diet, day in and day out, year after year over the course of a laissez-faire lifetime.

Throughout this process of degeneration, the mind takes refuge in areas of the body that can sustain it, and where the body fails to maintain an environment healthy enough for the mind to remain, it continues to pull back. Pesticides are designed to kill. This is their singular purpose. They eradicate. They destroy. The body is an organism that responds to poisons like any other organism: it begins to swiftly fail upon their unmediated ingestion. The pesticides we consume in small amounts each day are the same pesticides that more promptly kill insects and plants, the primary targets. It takes a little longer for the body to die but it inevitably will, for that is the nature of the poisons we ingest. Before death, we get the depressions, the anxieties, the autisms and Parkinsons, the cancers and aught malignancies and the many demise-inducing malfunctions. Then, in natural course, death. But our lives before our dyings are wholly compromised by the compounds of industry, which years ago were somehow allowed to be showered upon our foods.

Mind through all of these maladies is in constant retreat from a body hard-pressed to support it, and we can only begin the rather quick process of returning to health when our awareness steps in to reclaim its charge. This is what we are doing by choosing to eat exclusively organic, or more specifically food and drink untainted with pesticides.

Once you've committed to eating exclusively organic foods, your body will quickly begin the natural and all-too essential process of healing itself. Remarkably, within days of 'going clean' a physiological realigning and a literal recombining of the organism will commence. For those of you born after the 1990s, this will likely be the first time in your life the body you inhabit will begin to function as it was born to do, newly unencumbered by industrial compounds that have no other purpose than to kill.

Needless to say, this initial period of cleansing is one where you should take it slow and be entirely caring with yourself. Be attentive to all your bodily needs, including the need for rest, but also be sure to drink plenty of clean, filtered water to help flush the body of its decades' worth of stored toxins now in steady release. Eat fresh organic greens for straight-from-the-earth sustenance, especially dark leafy greens to allow for cellular respiration to re-oxygenate the body and blood. Eat fresh organic fruit to help lift the inner eye, restore clarity, elevate energy and even brighten temporarily dark moods. Eat lightly so the body, too, can focus its energies more on detoxifying than digesting meals that are perhaps larger or heavier than need be. Again, the mantra here is to go slow and take it easy on yourself. Give yourself at least a month, if not a few more, for any sense of full regeneration and feelings of renewal to find root. In this period, expect to feel some discomfort, tiredness, lack of motivation, seeming depressions, a general malaise, gaseousness, amongst other notable symptoms of detoxification.

Before long, all of these symptoms will begin to wane and a more enlivened sense of being will return in ways you've perhaps not experienced in years, if ever. Until then, it's best to rest often and sleep as much as your schedule will allow. Avoid television, if at all possible, especially the news, since both television and the 'news' it conveys has its own psychic toxicity which envenomates the mind, much as industrial pesticides poison the body. To that end, be like the mother wolf who, with noble ferocity, protects her ailing pup from predacious huntsmen who want nothing other than to turn that pup into a fur hat. For though the agri/media giants don't necessarily want you dead, they're not in the business of seeing you healthy, either. Their preference, in fact, is that you are borderline sickly, marginally stricken, and ever at the edge of desolation and despair. This gives their goods greater value, as well as a receptive market, for in this state you're in ontological want and a waiting vessel for the unabating delivery of their infinite wares. Be not their vessel but the noble wolf and protect your body and beautiful mind from the corporate conglomerates who view you as mere top-hat upon their earth-ravening returns.

While in the passing shadow of salutary return, it is best not to begin official practice on recognizing the nature of your own mind because both the body and the mind will be at odds with the task. Instead, the time is ripe for the preparatory work that will lead you toward recognizing mind essence. Beyond simple, this first practice toward regeneration is also entirely delightful, in that the focus is very much on the body with the intention of returning consciousness back into the whole. It is considered preparatory for future mind training because in order to recognize the nature of your own mind, mind itself must be fully present in the body. The mind, however, has difficulty remaining present when the body it abides in is compromised.

And so we've set ourselves on the road to healing, and it is essential we remain committed to this worthy endeavor. During this short transitional period, truly make every effort you can to allow the body, and with it the mind, to thoroughly cleanse and begin to heal. Consider it a long-deserved retreat. Meditation during this period should be more geared toward resting the body and objectively observing its daily changes, its small yet vital awakenings. Practice, if you do decide to meditate, in short sessions where the focus is on calming or easing exercises, such as following the breath, focusing on an object, or internally reciting a mantra. Any one of these individual practices help cut through both mental clutter and mind chatter.

For now, I'll advise against the practice of attempting to recognize your own mind in its natural state, since this advanced practice requires a clear, stable, and relatively luminous mind-space which, frankly, you might not be able to attain while the body is going through its epic cleansing. Besides healing, the best practice we can do during this period – a practice that isn't a meditation proper and should rather be done while lying down – is returning consciousness to the body, and this will be detailed next.

Returning Light

Returning consciousness to the body is a practice you can do anywhere, at any time of day, but perhaps initially you begin by lying down in bed, either just prior to sleep or upon awaking in the morning.

Simply allow the body to relax and feel yourself settle into a very comfortable rest. If, going in, you're feeling any anxiety or stress within the body, merely look at it with your mind's eye and note where it seems to arise, either the general area – the torso, for instance – or perhaps it's somewhere specific like the area directly around the heart. Sense first the general area, then look with the inner eye directly at the source of discomfort.

You'll likely note that wherever you're looking, the seeming point of origin tends to vanish. This is normal and to be expected. Usually when we look at something straight-on it tends to disappear. Still, you might feel the pervasiveness of some disturbance nonetheless. If so, then give it a mental nod and say a welcoming hello, as if it were an old friend in the neighborhood whose front yard you're lazily passing by. Any pain or discomfort you're feeling in the body, do the same: a short, friendly acknowledgment of its existence and then move along. Breathe deeply into the body, so that all the body's mass and any of its perceived ailments receive their share of much needed oxygen.

Remember, everything you do during this period is for healing. You are nurturing yourself, taking care of yourself. You are not turning away from any area of the body that has a need, and signs of stress, anxiety, low-level discomfort or out-and-out pain are ways the body calls for your attention, as well as your care. Ignoring these calls, as if they were the voicings of troublesome ghosts, only gives them further power to haunt. So when looking at the body with your inner eye, acknowledge the presence of all, including these irksome characters that share in your mental space. You acknowledge their voice, which is how they are expressing themselves as stress or anxiety or pain. Then you offer the first of the natural palliatives: an expansive, restorative breath. See the breath as an actual offering of care, because you are offering it as much symbolically as you are literally taking in fresh, life-sustaining oxygen. Envision the air entering the door of internal experience, your own personal experience, and as a ritual offering it arrives as an inhaling breath to all within that might feel stifled or constricted. With mere breath, you symbolically give attention to the parts of yourself that haven't been so well attended to, at least not until now, and this initial offering of breath is but the first in a larger set of practices that will aim to alleviate whatever might be the cause of internal stresses or actual physical disorders.

The many causes for our body's discomfort come, as noted, from toxins in our foods, frequencies of foreboding media, finances, troubles at the job, and so much more. The list is long. But coupled with all of this is our lack of attention to the incredibly rich details of our lives in every moment. We miss these details because our awareness is habitually in wander, dependably absent from the here and now. And so following upon the initial blessings of taking in deep breaths, we now breathe in our own restorative awareness that perhaps for some time has not been present in the body. Here, we bring the awareness back in, bring it home, so to speak, so that its curative nature can help quicken our recovery and restore us back to holistic well-being.

You are now lying in presence, comfortable and relaxed, loose in every limb. In lying in presence, you are lying in your own present awareness. This, it should be acknowledged, is quite special, and up until now it is perhaps also quite rare. Be conscious of your own awareness. See it as an old friend newly in return from a long travel. Take a minute to truly experience yourself in this present awareness, which externally sees you lying flat. Perhaps you're in bed or on the couch, in your yard or at the beach. Wherever you are, now move that awareness more subjectively into the body and begin filling it from the tips of the toes to the top of the head. The aim is to bring consciousness into each and every part of the body so that it is totally filled with your awareness-presence, which is none other than the enlivening nature of your own innate mind. This is the same mind you will later set out to recognize as being eternal, imperishable, and the absolute essence of who you really are.

Begin by moving your mind's eye down into the toes and see the toes from the perspective of within – not from the perspective of the brain 'up there,' but actually inside each of the toes, 'down there.' Go down there with your awareness and mindfully rise up into the toes and see if you can get a feeling for them. Perhaps prior to doing this exercise you had no feelings about your feet whatsoever, and I mean this literally: you could not feel your feet because you never really thought about them, lest like so many other things about the body we feel them only when they ache. Rarely, though, do we feel our body as it is in the actual moment because the mind is generally elsewhere.

Here, you are actively bringing your awareness into your toes, and then into your feet so that the awareness itself begins to enliven both. Awareness has a way of warming them as well, and you might notice with your awareness fully present in the feet that they begin to flush with a kind-of warmth, like one might feel after a foot massage. This is something like a massage, though here it is with the fingers of awareness.

Begin moving your attention through the toes, through the feet, their soles, between the bones and under the skin, and allow your awareness to enter those feet and reclaim them, for the feet are very much a part of your psychic body, your energy body, your body of awareness, as much as they are a part of the actual physical body those feet daily support. Feel these feet not as you normally might, but with the awakening touch of consciousness.

As you first begin to do this exercise, you can spend a minute or more in each area you rest your awareness. Here with the feet you can spend as long as you'd like or as long as you need to actually begin *feeling* your awareness within each foot: not a mental feeling but a physical feeling generated by the animating nature of awareness. After you do this a few times, awareness rushes straight in, as will the feeling, and you can thereafter re-enliven the feet within seconds of sending your awareness there.

For now, take your time and enjoy this rare moment of being one with your feet. When ready, move your awareness into the ankles and feel those ankles in all their complexity. If you have trouble feeling the ankles directly, then dip down into the feet and move some of that mind energy up into the ankles so that the love is shared and the ankles are not left out. Keep, though, your attention on the ankles until you can actually feel something, perhaps the embering of an awakening or some tingling of warmth.

As you move upward, know that the awareness now abiding in the feet and ankles remains there, still receiving the full blessings of placed consciousness. To that end, awareness is boundless and all-pervasive, so even as you bring this same mindfulness up into the calves, its presence below the calves will remain ever-constant and will continue to radiate even as you open the range of mind into the legs.

In this moment, however, awareness hovers in the calves, where you move it through the muscles and circle it around the two bones, then continue to allow it to rise as water would rise in a vase. Water does not disappear from the bottom of the vase as it rises to the top; the bottom stays full even as the water lifts steadily highward. And so it is with consciousness, which is in full knowing of your feet, your ankles, your calves, and now it continues to rise into the knees, where these, too, begin to bathe in the luminosity of mind.

As it spreads through the knees, let consciousness settle into the ligaments and bones, below the cap, around the sides and behind the knee, and very much feel the mind – your own awareness, in other words – moving through and around this most industrious area of the body, which perhaps in this moment has its own well-earned, workman-like aches. Let awareness rest into these aches as well, so that it softens sharp jabs or low-lying pains and brings a general ease and alleviation to all.

From the knees down your consciousness fills the space, which is to say the space of your lower legs is full with the presence of your own mind. This consciousness is the essence of your being, the elemental nature of who you are, and while as a conceptual entity you are also your body, and are intimately bound with it, you are in essence not the body but the very awareness you are bringing into it right now.

Thus you continue, and in doing so you are not only enlivening the body but healing it as well, because illness and the body's many maladies have difficulty remaining, much less entering, when awareness is present within. And even when disturbances have long taken hold, they struggle to remain when the light of our awareness is directed their way. Look squarely on any place of pain and the pain itself takes lesser shape and communicates itself in diminished degrees. When awareness is ongoing – and this will occur more often as you progress in your practice – these disturbances begrudgingly back-out so that an abiding mindfulness inhabits the very regions that once were their refuge.

This awareness, by the way, is the same awareness that saw the dangers from without – the noxious pesticides and toxic media – and it made the decision to shut them out so as to no longer poison the flesh or run riot in mind. That same awareness now moves through the body. It is a 360-degree awareness that seals the full circle so that nothing harmful can either enter or therein remain. With no awareness as gatekeeper, toxins of every order enter from without; likewise, when our awareness is nowhere within, countless disorders take resident hold. Maintaining awareness in all directions closes that perilous loop, and health at every level is returned.

Unless your issues with health are genetic, eating exclusively whole organic foods will remedy virtually all that ails, including issues with weight, energy, mood, even perception, particularly issues with self perception. This comes as a direct result of an engaged awareness. Awareness alone, being conscious of everything you put into your body, restores both body and mind to near total health because it is now observant of the whole, including the wholeness of within.

From where your awareness is at the knees, let it rise into the upper legs and thighs, into the hips, through the groin and around the buttocks so that the entire region, from the buttocks and the groin and down into the feet, is feeling grounded and awake, enlivened by the essence of mind itself.

It is here, at the lower end of the spine, where the first of our seven major chakras is located: the root chakra. The root chakra is a key energy center of the body, and it is the one that grounds you energetically – roots you, as the name suggests – to the very earth itself. Feel for this earth energy within your awareness. Allow it to reveal itself by placing your mind directly at its source.

Chakras are important to become familiar with because in feeling them, in sensing their life-availing energies – whether that energy is sluggish or alacritous, whether the chakra itself feels wide open or seemingly shut – you can begin regulating them with your own awareness, even open them when they feel closed down. *Feel* this chakra if you are able, the root chakra. If in these early stages you are unable to feel it, don't worry, with continued practice you will. For now, let the awareness fill the space below the spine before moving it upward into the area of the lower stomach and back.

Note that you are simultaneously seeing and feeling your awareness move upward through the body, and as we leave the root chakra you see and simultaneously feel your awareness move up toward the naval. While here, take a moment to check-in with the lower section of the body to see if awareness is still present throughout. A mental glance at the feet, at the calves and knees, the buttocks and groin, is all that is needed. You'll likely notice that with a quick scan the presence of mind leaps immediately forward in these areas. Any place that feels empty, shine the light of awareness back in and re-enliven it with your mindful gaze.

Then return to the region of the lower stomach. Here you'll find the second of the seven major chakras, the sacral chakra, which lies just below the naval. It would be helpful, when thinking about the chakras, especially if you want to begin working with them, to look at a chart to see where each in the body are and what they align with in terms of your experience. You'll find these charts everywhere online. With the sacral chakra, as with all of them, laying your awareness on this energy center is like laying your hands directly on the belly. Our chakras respond to our awareness much as the body responds to touch: with absolute love!

Awareness, like little fingers of light, feels for the energy of the chakra so as to become more aligned with it, and in knowing of it. With practice, you'll note energetically that the chakras will convey frequencies much more intimately, intensely, and engagingly than how other areas of the body respond when awareness is placed there. You might not be able to distinguish the difference the first few times you practice this exercise, but the more you bring awareness into the body the more your chakras will speak to you, and they can indeed be quite communicative.

The body thus far is half full with purposeful awareness, with presence of mind, and you continue to let it rise into the entire torso so that one-pointed awareness imbues the totality of its space. But while still in the sacral region, become conscious of the vital organs here as well. These organs not only maintain our good health, they also keep us lastingly alive. They are the kidney, spleen, pancreas, and intestines, all of which may be suffering and in need of your attention due to years of trying to cleanse away the accumulated poisons. The gluten allergies, the dairy allergies, the too-numerous-to-count other allergies that come with a diet saturated in pesticides and the incessant intake of GMO-concocted foods can do this area particularly grave harm. The stomach feels this most prominently, as will the kidneys. Bring awareness into each of these organs and let them know your intention is to heal them as well.

Moving up from the sacral chakra you'll come upon the solar plexus chakra, also known as the sun chakra, and this chakra lives up to its name in that it has the ability to bring in clarifying light: if light is something you equate with confidence, security, identity, a more spacious self. But this chakra is likewise an essential lightway into the heart chakra. If your aim is to open your heart chakra, you must enter through an open solar plexus chakra, so bringing awareness to this chakra is essential to opening your heart as well, to, say, love, compassion, joy, healthy relationships. If the solar plexus chakra is 'closed,' so to speak, then the heart chakra is likely in the same condition. With this one exercise of bringing awareness into the body, you can begin opening these spirit centers and get them flowing energetically, the way the energy field of the universe needs them to be, the way your own healthy body and mind need them to be.

Also be aware of a key organ in this area, the liver. The liver cleanses the blood and breaks down the litany of toxins we take in, including the intoxicants of alcohol and drugs and the compounds taken in through diet that do us endless harm. Bringing awareness into the liver is a necessary salve for an organ that works tirelessly toward keeping us fresh so that both body and mind function at their very best. Take the liver into the hand of awareness and be tender with your mindful touch.

Around the area of the heart, an organ we equate with the beat of life itself, you'll feel the heart chakra, perhaps the most talkative of all our chakras once you're in relationship to it. How do you strike up this relationship? By doing this very exercise – by bringing awareness into the fullness of your body and into each of the seven chakras specifically. See with the mind's eye your awareness entering the heart chakra. Allow the inner vision to move through it, since the heart indeed is a throughway chakra and has its insightful eye on all things, both internally and externally. Allow your awareness to rest in the center of this all-seeing chakra and observe it as being the leading light in your spiritual body, for it assuredly is. See the heart chakra as being not only an open kingdom to your physical body, your energy body and your spiritual self, but also as being entirely one with the space that exists around your body. The heart chakra inhabits this space, too, which is how it can feel the truth of what's around us well before the intellect can.

You are now seeing the heart chakra as being spacious, receptive, and communicative, yet the heart chakra is also the wisdom keeper of all that you have ever known. Not the mundane, everyday minutia of your routine life but the highest knowings of your timeless Being. Visualize no blockages when entering your heart with awareness, though if you really can't shake the feeling that the 'heart is blocked,' as is the common expression, then caress it each day with consciousness, with the gentle eye of awakening, and slowly begin the process of softening it up, creating tiny yet essential openings into the perceived blockage until you actually begin to feel something akin to an energetic buzzing. When you start feeling this, focus only on that, not the remaining blockage, and let your awareness nourish the new growth so that, on its own, it creates a larger and larger opening for this most amazing energy organ to do its job. To that end, when this one chakra is open you'll have a new helmsman at the head of your journey into the essence of mind, because the heart wants nothing more than to be in the presence of awareness. Later, when you find yourself resting in the natural state, you'll also find the heart is truly an organ, one that makes incredibly lovely music in perfect harmonics with the nature of all existence.

And please know that whatever trauma you've experienced in this life which may have your heart seemingly shut down, your own intimate awareness filling it each day will certainly re-open it, will bring it animatedly back to life. This I say from experience. Give it time, be patient and remain positive, lay your loving awareness on this chakra again and again and it will surely awaken, and likely sooner than you might think possible. Its nature is openness, and to naturally express this openness it awaits only your permission, and your attention.

From the area of the heart, continue to move your awareness around your back and through your chest, around your ribs, your lungs, and then bring it up into your shoulders where here, instead of going straight up into the head, let your awareness move down into the arms, into the palms of each hand, into the fingers, and fill the entire space so that everything below the head is alive and aware, filled with consciousness, with the thrumming presence of mindfulness.

By now awareness is almost self-lifting, self-enlarging, but you lead it anyhow so that your inner eye arrives in the area of the throat, and you fill this space, too. Here, you have your fifth major energy center, the throat chakra, which has its evident connection to self-expression and communication. If you've had trouble with your voice, communicating your needs or speaking the truth about who you are, it is likely your throat chakra needs your attention. If so, then bringing more awareness to this area will open the channel for clearer, more confident self-expression.

From the throat and throat chakra, lift your awareness up through all areas of the head, beginning with the bottom of the chin, the jaw, the lips, mouth, tongue, cheeks, eyes, temples, back of the head, forehead, top of the scalp. While in this region, bring your awareness into the last two of the seven major chakras: the forehead or third-eye chakra, and then the crown chakra at the top of your skull. The third-eye, or sixth chakra, is considered the eye of intuition, of implicit or instinctual knowing, whereas the crown chakra connects you to spirit, to the wisdom of the universe, to higher guides, and it is through this last chakra that your own spirit will depart when it leaves your body at death.

All the chakras are connected in ways that keep the energy body unified and moving in healthful equilibrium, so it is important to keep the chakras open, receptive, and activated. Bringing your awareness into each of them individually helps tremendously in keeping them responsive to the environment in and around your physical body, but it helps stabilize your energetic and emotional well-being as well.

Your entire body now sings with consciousness, and with frequent practice this exercise should take no more than five or ten minutes, depending on how long you want to spend in any one area of the body. But once the body becomes more responsive, each session may take only a few minutes to bring consciousness into the fullness of self. In doing this, you will remediate many of the destabilizing issues you experience in your life. Combine this with the follow-up practices we're about to discuss and you'll look back in less than a year to see an individual who has wholly transformed.

Beginning with this one exercise is a beautiful first step in an awakening that I'm certain for you, as for so many of us, has long been sought.

The Fourth Time

Every thought, every sound, every thing that passes through your sight takes place in the present. Scan the gaze in any direction and you'll not find a past. You see only the nowness of this ongoing present. Scan again the attendant gaze and you'll not find a future, either, for there is still only this very present. The present is, well, present in every instance of our lives.

Looking directly at the present, particularly as we observe it through the lens of our practice, we see the definitive absence of any past, and minus a past there can be no opposite. Like the very space we exist in, which goes absolutely nowhere in terms of time, our lives are happening at no other moment than the here and now, a seamless, ceaseless present which holds not even a notion of variable time, for the notion itself exists only in conceptual mind.

That being said, if you were to sit down and actually look for this present moment through analysis, as is done in quantum physics and in high meditation, you would find there is not even a present moment. There is only what is known as 'the fourth time,' which is no time, not even a quantifiable present. You can find this time in two ways on your own: one, through mindful observation, or what in later chapters will be called 'insight mediation,' while the other means of seeing the fourth time is through 'direct perception.'

The first way of recognizing the fourth time is through insight meditation, where you simply observe our so-called present in its ticking of the now. Laying your discerning eye of awareness directly on it, you find irrefutably that no present moment exists, that 'present' is but a designation we lay on an idea that is empty of itself.

The other way of arriving at this fourth time is experientially, and this is done through recognizing mind in its natural state, then resting there. In this resting, what we experience through direct perception is a timeless, spacious, ongoing nowness that is not a present but a *presence*, and it is this presence we in our natural state always exist in. It is of the kind, this presence, that is the essence of our eternal being and the culmination of all the higher teachings we've been gifted to practice.

And so we do just that: we practice.

The Practice

Points on Alignment

Posture: Sitting upright in what is known as the 'seven-point meditation posture' is the ideal position for experiencing progress in practice. The upright sitting position allows for the body's energy winds to flow freely within, whereas in lying down, sitting angled or gangly, the natural movement of our internal winds are slowed or even interrupted because the channels they move through are bent or compressed. This is an unnecessary hinderance to our meditation before we've even begun, since compressed channels and obstructed winds create conditions antithetical to finding stillness, let alone clarity of mind. The thinking mind cannot settle, discursive thoughts continue to distract, tranquility is not easily maintained, and any opportunity for recognizing our naturally occurring mind is likely lost.

Sitting upright in the seven-point pose allows for the earth below and the sky above to help ground and stabilize the energies within the body. The grounding energies of the earth literally root the energies of the body through the root chakra, and the open sky-energies above the crown chakra help bring clarity and spaciousness to the perceiving mind. Between the two chakras, the root and the crown, there is a straight, unobstructed channel connecting all the chakras. The easy flow between them brings stability to the mind-body energies on the whole, allowing them to more readily settle and giving us the best opportunity to recognize mind in its natural state.

The upright position has us sitting with our back straight – the traditional analogy is to an arrow or a stack of gold coins: our spine should be this straight. The chin should be slightly tilted toward the chest, tongue resting lightly against the palate, mouth either barely closed or slightly open, and we breathe easily, restfully through the nose. The hands lie lightly upon the lap, either one on top of the other or loosely side by side. The hands can also be resting on the knees or cupping into the upper thighs – whatever is comfortable. Legs are crossed, again, so that it is comfortable. If the knees or feet begin to ache and thereby distract, stretch them fully out in front so that the legs are together, straight, uncrossed; remain, however, sitting upright from the waist up. For extra support, you can rest the back against a wall, and for even more support a soft pillow can be placed at the lower back.

Duration: Transcendental Meditation, a practice I'll speak briefly to in the next chapter, has a good framework for how long meditations should last, and how often. They suggest meditating twice daily, once in the morning and once in the afternoon or early evening, 20 minutes each session. This is a great starting point. That being said, there really is no set duration for the time we should ideally practice. If 20 minutes is the time needed to arrive at mindfulness and remain in the full presence of awareness, this is good. Better still is arriving at a stable awareness which allows for the recognition of mind essence, our own natural state, and if this takes 20 minutes then all the better. A pattern you do not want to fall into is setting a time for 20 minutes, or any duration for that matter, only to drift for the entire session in mindless distraction. This, clearly, would not be good. On the other hand, if you are wanting to truly excel in understanding and inhabiting the wisdom teachings on mind, then it is likely you will practice more often and for longer durations. This would indeed be excellent. I suggest allowing for at least an hour per session, once you feel you've been able to recognize mind essence, since learning how to stabilize in the natural state, and become intimately familiar with it, pretty much demands this kind of liberal allowance of time, which will equate in even greater measure to an appreciable enlivening of your awareness and a swift, almost certain movement toward realization. But twice a day, 20 minutes per session is great for getting started and generating a beneficial rhythm.

The Eyes: In Dzogchen we typically practice with the eyes open, though this by no means is a hard and fast rule. To do this comfortably, and with stability, we must begin by training in shamatha, a practice I will speak to in the next chapter. If you've trained in shamatha, then continue in your practice as you have been – eyes either opened or closed depending on the circumstance. If you are unacquainted with shamatha, then I suggest initially meditating with your eyes closed, since without training in stabilizing the mind with your eyes open, it can be difficult to practice without falling swiftly into distraction.

Breath: Focusing on your breath, without forcing it into a particular rhythm, is a great way to relax, and for that reason alone it is a worthy technique. 'Focusing,' however, does not mean mentally gazing directly at the breath. Rather, it means merely being aware of the breath amongst everything else we are present with in our meditation practice. A more structured breath technique is included in the several variations of shamatha practice used to still the thinking mind, and this indeed is an essential practice when the aim is to ultimately recognize the natural state. If you are using the breath as part of a larger body of practices to help stabilize and prepare for the recognition of mind essence, then do continue. I'll recommend a different version of shamatha in the next chapter, one where the focus is on an object other than the breath. But meditation is a very personal practice, so whatever technique works best for you in quieting the clamorous mind is likely the correct technique for you.

Mantra: Yes, per the lineage you associate your mantras with and in accordance with your traditional practice. As it pertains to mind recognition training, however, no mantra is used when recognizing mind in its natural state.

Music or Generated Background Sound: No. This is not something you want to artificially add into mind recognition training. The natural and industrial sounds already existent in the world are soundscapes enough for our practice, and we needn't introduce any more (or less).

Aids in Our Arrival

There are two practices that will aid you in the recognition of your own mind in its natural state. One is a traditional technique, and is in fact a mandatory one in terms of preparing for Dzogchen instruction. But even if mind recognition is not your ultimate goal, this first practice is a reliable way of quieting the mind whenever you need it to instantly settle. The other practice might be considered alternative in the context of Dzogchen, but it, too, is an excellent technique so I'll briefly speak to it here.

The first of these two practices is known as shamatha, and its purpose is to help stabilize the otherwise unruly, unstable, insatiable, interminably restless mind. Shamatha requires two things: your focused attention and an object to lay your attention on. Early in my practice I was instructed to find a pebble or small rock, and I particularly liked this because the object was from the natural world. But you can also use a small statue of a Buddha if you'd prefer, or an image of a goddess or even the letter A from the alphabet: any smallish object conveniently at hand will work.

Set it out a few feet in front of you as a support for the gaze, as a scaffold, of sorts, for steadying awareness so that attention doesn't stray or get dragged away with each arising thought. To where might awareness leave us with the passing of thought? Everywhere other than the present moment, and it is here in this moment that shamatha teaches you to remain, with tight focus on the rock which is presently before you.

Shamatha is an age-old practice to help settle the mind. Its active, singular focus narrows awareness into a one-pointed rest. Distractions are few, including the distraction of thought, because our eye on the pebble is conscious, engaged, and fixed. We begin by setting our intention to remain one with the object, with awareness intently on-point and unwavering. If the mind does wander, which it inevitably will, a quick reminder has our focus back on the rock.

Note the word 'intention.' Setting the intention to remain focused at the beginning of each practice leads to the reminder when you eventually drift, and the reminder brings you back to an attentive focus on the rock. Beginning each practice with intention is important, and in doing this your skill in remaining mindful will quickly develop.

The body is relaxed. The eyes are relaxed. The focus on the rock is sharp, tight, and there is just enough firmness in the gaze to hold it steady. There is also the ability to increase or decrease the tension in this firmness so the gaze remains unwaveringly on the rock, just as one would tighten and loosen the tension on a guitar string so it stays on that perfect note.

Playing with the tension in this way, and becoming skillful at it, allows for a slow release of this same tension when there is confidence your awareness is well balanced and will not stray. At that point, awareness is allowed to merely rest on the rock without any effort in holding it there. You will feel this looseness in awareness when it arrives, since in that moment you'll experience all things within the instance of stillness, including the rock, are in absolute balance. Nothing pulls the attention one way or another, not even a thought, but nothing within our vision, either, which in its state of perfect equilibrium opens beyond the rock to include all in the clarity of a vision now stable and vividly aware.

It is a sign of good progress when you often arrive at stability, but the real progress occurs in that significant shift when awareness no longer holds itself stably on the rock; rather, the rock now rests unwaveringly in awareness. This shift in perspective is from a subject-object duality to a stable and spacious singularity, a oneness, where all that is resting in our field of vision is now one within awareness, within a no-subject-no-object space. When this occurs regularly, and the experience is dependably stable, we can then let go of the rock as our support for this practice and move on to space itself, where no rock nor any other objects are needed to help stabilize our awareness.

In removing the rock, which to this point has been set out a few feet in front of you, you now shift the focus ever so slightly so that your gaze is lifted to the space above where the rock once sat, and now that tight area of space becomes the new point of focus. You hold our attention here, in this emptiness of space, in the same way you held it on the rock, and when you arrive in your practice where holding the gaze is with an effortless ease and is reliably steady – the space you rest in is no longer 'tight' but easily and evenly open – then you are now ready to move on to the more advanced practice of *recognizing* the space you now so effortlessly abide in: this being the unwavering space of intrinsic mind.

In Tibet, back in the day, the guru would have his students wear a colorful powder on their eyelashes so that if they blinked during shamatha training it would be clear to the guru who was doing the practice correctly and who was not. Students who blinked during practice would wear a lovely speckling of color around their eyes, and those who did not remained as plain and unadorned as when they began. Our aim in this practice is for the latter, though this too takes training, so be patient with yourself and do find joy in all your small successes, and pleasure still in what might be considered the smaller failures, of which there is nothing of the kind.

While developing and attaining some stability with shamatha, I'll also recommend a secondary practice known as Transcendental Meditation. I say 'secondary' because TM has nothing to do with formal Dzogchen instruction, but it is an effective technique in delivering all levels of practitioners, both beginning and advanced, directly to the source, and it does this quite quickly within a meditation session, where the practitioner can then get a view on what the natural state looks like.

In Transcendental Meditation, the arrival at stillness ironically occurs through movement. The TM practitioner is given a personalized mantra, and it is through the internal, mental repetition of this mantra that the chatter of thinking mind is penetrated, allowing us to momentarily enter an opening that is utter, a stillness that feels absolute. Here, we have the rare opportunity to perceive and experience our own ground-level awareness, what TM calls the Unified Field.

The term Unified Field has a rather mystical ring to it, as if the enlightened space it alludes to were elsewhere, beyond our actual selves. The proposed idea is that the recitation technique, reciting the mantra, allows us entry into the Unified Field through the nethers of our own unexplored mind, where we therein transcend. This is and is not the case, dialectically speaking, for we can indeed access this so-called Field by employing the conceptual technique of our mantra as a way in. The Unified Field, however, is not beyond the mind nor is it anything other than mind, in that it is not something mystical and it is certainly not far off. To the contrary, the Unified Field is space itself, albeit infused with awareness, and it is this very emptiness of space in which our own innate mind eternally exists. The Unified Field is everywhere around us and entirely within us, and it is enlivened not only by our own awareness but by a sea of sentience which is the sum of us all.

Look at the space before you and you are looking at the Unified Field. Look at the space inside your mind and you are looking at the Unified Field. Space does not stop at the skin of your body. It extends through everything, permeates everything, including the totality of the body within. Our mind inhabits this same space. Beyond the emptiness of space the mind cannot be found, for there is no 'beyond space' since space is everywhere. Mind is a presence in space, is inseparable from it. We'll see later that mind cannot be found within the body proper: not in the legs nor in the hands, in the heart or in the head. Rather, mind abides in the very space that fills the body through.

When the body dies, the brain remains as dead matter in the corpse. The mind will not be found there upon our death, nor will there be remnants of awareness still lingering in the skull. And though it seems from our conceptual perspectives that the body houses the mind and that mind-function takes place specifically in the head, it is really the case that the body gravitationally grounds the mind in our temporal flesh, and our awareness, were the body to suddenly fall dead, would be immediately released into surrounding space, the same space we walk through and sleep in, the same space we look across to muse upon the inconstant moon, the day-bearing sun and the glittering wonders of the universe beyond. The mind is nowhere, not even now, other than in this space, for that space moves without interruption through the entire body within.

The Unified Field, then, should not be seen as something mystical or Other, or even a beyond we must transcend into. And while 'transcending' is a lovely word to describe the experience taking place in Transcendental Meditation, what really is happening is our own conceptual minds are being cleared of their concepts, the thoughts are being cut directly through by the mantra. This allows entry into our own naturally occurring mind, our ground-level awareness, which opens before us and in this opening we are given a brief moment to experience it directly. This feels like transcendence, but it is really more of an unveiling, a revealing of our own natural state which is always present within us. We are never without it.

Innate mind, our natural state, is an open, ongoing emptiness that is the ever-conveying source of our conceptual selves. When entering and observing it in meditation, we see its emptiness with our own awareness, which itself is inseparable from the emptiness we are in witness of. It is this combination of emptiness and awareness that can be called, if you like, the Unified Field, but in truth the Field is nothing other than the commingling of awareness and space, cognizance and emptiness. This is our natural state, the actual essence of who we are as an eternal, singular awareness which itself is one, or unified, with all. The TM technique gives us short entry into this space of awareness before conceptual mind kicks us out, wherein the mantra is returned to and we recite again until we find ourselves back in the natural state.

TM, then, has us dipping in and out of the natural state. Shamatha practice, on the other hand, teaches us to settle and still our awareness, then stabilize and importantly *relax* in that stillness so we have time to recognize our own mind in its natural state without too quickly leaving it. The training is considered foundational in that it prepares us for the more advanced Dzogchen instructions which, after recognizing, have us comfortably resting in the natural state without distraction.

Shamatha is a practice we develop proficiency in over time, so that at some point we own it, much as we would own any of our other developed abilities – learning to walk as a baby, for instance, or riding a bike as a child, cooking an elaborate meal as an adult without need of a recipe. And as with those three examples, the experiential *knowing* does not occur until we first learn the method, then we practice until the knowing becomes intrinsic – in other words, we no longer think about it. We just do.

After learning shamatha you will no longer be frustrated by a mind that won't stop thinking, that won't quiet itself no matter what's thrown at it. Rather, upon the quiet recognition of the mind gone amok, the practice settles it straight-out so that it falls still like a kitten in its mother's tender mouth, with her tooth of awareness softly in its neck.

TM works more like a bat echolocating through a darkened cave. The cave being your mind, with its walls of identity and thought so seemingly solid, while the echolocation of the bat being the mantra bouncing off its conceptual walls like sound off slabs of stone, so that the heretofore unseen, unknown openings into the cavernous mind within can be revealed.

Sounding off and thereby avoiding hard contact with the cavern walls, the bat makes a straight shot through darkness into the warming chambers within, where it will rest and rejuvenate after a night chasing bugs on the lifting winds, much as we, after chasing thought on the tireless winds of mind, are similarly in need of a re-inspiriting rest. TM gives us this, but it also offers us something of far greater value: the opportunity to experience our own natural mind in the space the technique has opened for us, and this is the precious jewel it has waiting for us each time we 'transcend.'

The Cat of Shamatha and The Bat of Trans-Med, two creatures of night as our sovereign guides through the darkened terrains of conceptual mind. The cat, remaining magnificently still for moments on end, will take unaware the mark of its eye and still it apace. While the bat, ever alacritous in the air, wings itself eyeless into the subterranean depths where it hangs in the stillness to reanimate afresh. Take these two as totem and you will surely receive their inborn wisdoms, their bearings and dispositions, so you can embody each in your practice which itself marks its eye on mind in its natural state.

The combination of shamatha practice and TM is a nice one, and I encourage you to employ both techniques over a period of at least a few months before diving into the less structured, and thereby potentially more problematic practices of Dzogchen. I say 'problematic' because for Dzogchen to be truly meaningful, and effective, the mind must be stable enough, still enough, fluid enough and open enough to even put the teachings into contextual practice without unknowingly heading down the wrong path. Steady the mind first, calm it through shamatha training, and only then move ahead into the more profound and transformative wisdom teachings of the Great Perfection.

The Transmission

A word about receiving Dzogchen instruction from a qualified master, specifically as it pertains to the mind transmission which points out our own natural state: frankly, you must, and when I say *you must,* I am speaking in reference to *most* individuals attempting to become familiar with this profound practice. Some individuals, those who are more naturally inclined or with exceptionally high capacity, can merely read the teachings on the page and they are solidly on their way. But for the rest of us, it is important to receive these teachings firsthand, direct from the mouth of a master, even if it's only every so often, for those occasionally direct transmissions will bring clarification and a depth of experience like no book can.

I grew up in Los Angeles, a city few Dzogchen masters ever set foot in. Tenzin Wangyal Rinpoche regularly did, and to him I am eternally grateful for those years he made LA a place of enlightened practice. Other great masters had their community of students in San Francisco, Colorado, Canada, Mexico, Italy, to name the few I knew of, and whenever I could afford it I would travel to these places to receive the teachings directly. I did three-day retreats, ten-day retreats, took copious notes, then came back to LA and meditated on those teachings, considered them, analyzed them, read through and referred constantly to my notes, read these same masters again through their books to find words of clarifying wisdom and even clarification on ideas I didn't quite understand. And then out on the road I'd go again to receive more follow-up teachings, further transmissions directly from the source, and I did this for many years.

It works, this kind of multi-portal entry into the teachings, and it works exceptionally well as one way, though not the historically ideal way, of receiving instruction/transmissions from our living masters. And for those of us here in the West, with our lives moving in so many different directions, it is pretty much the only way.

Wherever you live there will be a great teacher either in your city or your country or a country very near sometime this year. Book yourself in, and see your journey toward the teachings as being in direct line with the great pilgrimages of old, where pilgrims then and still today travel sometimes *weeks* to be present at the very feet of their sought-for sage, their noble master, a shaman or sculpted saint. That is to say, please don't let any sense of isolation thwart your quest for insight into your own mind, and don't let the perception of distance come between you and the development of your own practice. Even if you're able to receive a single teaching from one true master each year, or once every few years, you should make this happen. The teacher would love for you to be a part of the community, known as the sangha, and the community will be most gracious in welcoming you in. Then return to the comfort of your own home, refresh your experience by reading their teachings on the page, and practice practice practice. The rewards, you'll find, are truly immeasurable.

The Natural State

When preparing to enter your mind and recognize it in its natural state, begin the meditation by sitting upright in traditional meditative pose: legs crossed, back straight, chin slightly tilted to the chest, hands resting comfortably in your lap. As you continue with this practice, you can certainly do it with your eyes open, and in Dzogchen practice this is the norm. Here, I suggest practicing with the eyes closed until you've gained confidence in recognizing mind essence and are stable in resting there.

Another clarifying point is this: if your one practice thus far has been Transcendental Meditation and you've had no training in stabilizing the mind through shamatha practice, then your mantra will surely take you in to that awakened space we aim to recognize, but you will remain there far too briefly for any recognition to be fully realized before thoughts again arise and you find yourself back on the mantra. If mind is on the mantra, it cannot recognize itself, let alone rest in that recognition.

This is why we need shamatha training, so that we remain stable in this awakened space, observe it at our leisure, recognize it as our own naturally occurring mind, then rest in this recognition for way longer than the TM technique on its own allows. When you've spent more time in the experience of recognition, are both stable in this recognition and confident the mind you are looking at is your own – not something else entirely – then TM is a good technique to use at will.

And so you sit, settle both the body and mind, then consciously let everything go before attempting to recognize mind in its natural state. The fable that began this book was no mere storytelling. The mandate there, to let go of everything including the stories of yourself, is essential, and a basic precept for entering the mind. There can be no tales going in, including any and all stories attached to your identity. Narratives of who you are, your history, your various operating personas – mother, son, artist, addict, enabler, victim, divorcee, teacher, spiritual seeker – none of these mean anything in innate mind. They're empty concepts even prior to entering the natural state, and seen from the perspective of innate mind they truly become something indescribably absent, vacant – indeed, *empty* – of substance or any significance. They mean nothing, so let your attachment to them slip away right from the start.

Sit with the high intention of entering a sacred space – your own mind – and see this space as being utterly absent of all conceptual underpinnings. Here, you'll look through its naked essence to experience the emptiness as being your natural own. You'll recognize this essence when you observe nothing other than a wide-open, unfabricated, crystalline awareness free from the many occurrences that normally have it awash – thoughts, feelings, scenarios, et al.

As you enter the naked space of your own naturally occurring mind – 'naked' in that it is starkly stripped of concepts or constructs of any kind – you will begin to develop a familiarity with its characteristic emptiness, and in time you'll come to know it as being your own mind beneath the mind – the non-conceptual beneath the conceptual – for other than awareness, that which sees the emptiness, there is nothing else that defines this space, save for its capacity to allow all appearances to arise within it.

With continued practice, particularly as a result of your shamatha training, you'll be able to rest in this emptiness while observing it with an entirely at ease awareness, being both steady and relaxed. In this resting, you'll begin seeing the utter luminosity of awareness itself, as well as its omniscience – its ability to see even itself. This is key to Dzogchen practice: being aware of your own awareness being aware, or awareness seeing itself. In time, you'll recognize this as being none other than an observance of your own mind, a mind that transcends body and is wholly one with the space it exists in.

In the early stages of your practice this initial recognition will be laced with some uncertainty. In other words, mind essence will be seen, and your sense of it will be one of familiarity, but questions regarding perspective will inevitably arise, such as, "is this it?" or "is this my mind or am I looking at something else?" This uncertainty is inevitable and entirely normal.

When receiving the mind transmission from a master – getting the pointing out instructions directly from the source – the master will ask you a series of questions which will require brief responses. You'll recall those questions from the first chapter's pointing out. 'Pointing out' literally means the master points out, or points you toward the recognition of your own mind essence, allowing you to see it clearly, nakedly, in its natural state. The pointing out, then, is a direct introduction to innate mind. But of equal importance is the affirmation your guru brings to your experience in this moment of seeing, in that he or she confirms what you're seeing is indeed your own naturally occurring mind and not something other.

When going into these meditations while still trying to recognize, have those same questions you read in the first chapter hovering in your awareness so you can consider them in the moment. In other words, when looking at something within mind that appears to be its essence – empty yet vividly aware – you can loosely float a question that might help clarify what you're seeing. For instance, does this mind I'm looking at have a beginning or an end? From where does it arise and to where does it go? Is it close to me or far away? Is it an object? Does it have a shape or dimension?

These questions do not come up so much as a thought but as a guiding voice, and they arise in mind without any attachment to an answer or without the question itself disrupting or disturbing the empty state you are witnessing. In practicing this way, you yourself become the wise master within the space of your own mind. But be aware of your own ego as well, which loves to step in and pull you alluringly away from the mind you're attempting to know. It will do this with flattery if distraction itself is failing. It can have you patting yourself on the back or, worse, encouraging you toward overconfidence, even arrogance. This is an unfortunate though entirely predictable misstep for many, so be cognizant of the wiliness of ego, especially if you see this as being a trait within yourself – that of self-inflation. Remember, the ego is not your friend, though it is not your enemy, either. It, simply put, is interminably there, an entity born of its own imaginings and embroiled wholly in the conceptual state, so you'll have to contend with it to varying degrees until you're fully knowing of the natural state.

To that end, continue to reference the Dzogchen teachings in order to clarify any points or any experience that might lead to misunderstanding or easily send you down the wrong path. Know, also, that Dzogchen practice demands regular clarification as well as a healthy recalibration of how you're perceiving all that arises in your experience, which is why conferring with a master is important. But if no master is available, then carefully read their books. Read not just the words on the page but the space between the words, i.e., the spirit of those words and the ideas they allude to, and pay particular attention to the metaphors these masters employ, for it is particularly these metaphors that take you closer to enlightened meaning than the words themselves possibly can, since words in the end are products of conception and speak, per their own implicit function, almost solely to the conceptual state, for that is their natural domain.

What other questions might the wise old master ask of you as you look at mind in its natural state? He or she might pose the question, "In looking at your resting mind, who is it that is at rest? Where is this resting taking place? What is the nature of this resting? That which is resting, does it have a shape? a color? a location? Is it a thing, or is it nothing?" To the latter, your answers could only be in the negative, meaning no shape or color or location can be found. Nor is there any *thing* to be seen other than emptiness. The master may ask, "In the emptiness you are observing, is there still a knowing, an awareness which could be called an *is-ness* or a *such-ness*, or *that which is*?" If you are looking at mind in its natural state, then your answer will be, "Yes, there is *something* there, an *is-ness*, as you say, a knowing." And it would go on like this, with the questions put forward being very similar to the ones the departing sage presented to the pilgrim in the opening chapter. In short, there is nothing to be seen, and *we see this*. The nothing is our emptiness while the seeing is our awareness.

When sitting in meditation, you merely observe the space of empty mind to see, indeed – just as the master pointed out – it has no shape, no color, no location or destination. It has no inside or out, no up or down. There is no past when a past is directly looked for, and you'll find no future in it, either. There is no distance between you and it, this *is-ness* being witnessed by your knowing. And your knowing sees, also, there is nothing to be damaged or destroyed. It sees no creation or fabrication, and it sees this as direct perception through an awareness that innately knows. Your awareness also sees that this *is-ness* does not end, because when looking directly at it no ending will ever be found. *That which is* innate mind likewise has no identity, and so it cannot be named. You do not merely guess this, nor do you infer it; you actually *see* this in your own experience, and you see it through direct perception which arrives as nothing less than transcendent wisdom. In observing all of this, you rest in the recognition of it, and in that resting you become more and more familiar with it.

How do you become confident in knowing this mind? You first recognize it, and then you rest in it. Recognize and rest. Recognize and rest. Do this over and over and over. There will be no moment in this process when you'll ever get tired of it or bored, because what's happening is a direct tapping into the very source of your own eternal being, and no words can describe how truly wondrous this is, though, admittedly, in using the word 'wondrous' we arrive yet again at another concept. From the experiential perspective, the perspective of resting, there is, in truth, nothing 'wondrous' about it. Yet to describe it as 'ordinary,' as is often done by the masters, would appear from the conceptual perspective to be a grand understatement. How can it be *ordinary?* The word 'ordinary,' however, is perhaps the most apt description of what, from the perspective of the natural state, it inherently *is*, in that, indeed, *it is as it is*, and so, as has been said all along, it is an *is-ness*.

While resting in this *is-ness,* however wondrous or ordinary it may be, distraction inevitably occurs. Thoughts will arise. When this happens, merely remember to return to recognition, wherein again you see the natural state, you recognize it, and then you rest once more in the knowing of it. You do this again and again until short moments become longer moments and longer moments move into more stable states of ongoing realization. And this is the training. There is nothing more to it. This will be your entire practice going forward.

Equipoise

Having recognized the mind which has no origin, location, destination, or cessation, we now aim to seamlessly slip beyond mere 'looking' in order to arrive at what is traditionally called 'equipoise,' though it could easily be called 'the sweet spot' as well. This is the experience of being in absolute rest within mind, where there is nothing, not even the slightest low-level tension, tugging at our awareness, and the body itself, along with everything else, is in perfect equilibrium *within* awareness. Shamatha practitioners experience something similar to this when, if you recall, the rock is no longer the focus of awareness but instead rests in perfect equilibrium within awareness. This is known as 'effortless mindfulness,' where the rock becomes entirely one with all else within awareness.

Perception in effortless mindfulness is often alluded to by the Tibetan masters as being 'of one taste,' for all in the seeing is an experience of oneness. Transcendental Meditation practitioners are likely to experience equipoise at the perceived arrival into the Unified Field, wherein the mantra is released and the practitioner rests in stillness, in what feels like utter presence and peace. But the experience of equipoise is typically short-lived with TM, since thoughts again arise, the mantra is returned to and the cycle of recitation resumes.

It is this equipoise we refer to, after having recognized mind, that best defines the experience of *resting* in mind. We are told to first recognize, and then the instructions tell us to rest in the recognition. This is all we are being instructed to do: recognize the natural state, then rest in the recognition of it. If you have stabilized your awareness through shamatha practice, and if you've received the pointing out instructions from a master who points you toward all indicators of mind essence, then it is rather easy to recognize your own natural state going forward, wherein you rest and ultimately receive the very wisdoms our innate mind naturally imparts.

Regarding the above instructional 'pointing out,' know that you can recognize innate mind on your own, and many have without a master explicitly pointing it out to them. But in having only this kind of recognition – without, in other words, having it formally pointed out – there is a greater tendency toward doubt, and doubt is a problem in Dzogchen practice since essential to our progress is a *knowing*, a certainty, that "this mind I am looking at is my own." Confidence in seeing is important.

Still, if you feel you've recognized your own naturally occurring mind then it is likely you have, and you should carry on with your practice while trusting that what you're seeing is indeed your own mind (for whose else could it be?), and do this – develop, persevere, remain ever-cognizant of ego, your own story, any-and-all pitfalls that predictably, for you, tend to trip you up – until you're able to get confirmation and/or clarification from a qualified master. In the meantime, let the knowing of the recognition speak to you from a place of open awareness, which in itself should not have the quality of a subjective presence; there must only be an awareness presence, absent, and therefore empty, of any subjective, substantial, corporeal or in any way 'personal' sense of even itself.

After having recognized mind essence – which is a recognition of emptiness – it is the arrival at resting where things can be a bit tricky, in that the easy movement into a relaxed, wholly at rest state isn't always so easy. For example, you've just received the pointing out instructions from your master, and you return home to practice. You sit down to meditate and mentally allow the questions the master posed to you in the pointing out to float around in the mind. There they wait to offer guidance. And, indeed, you feel in this one meditation that recognition has been made. You are seeing within awareness that mind is not coming and going, that it is instead present and ongoing. It has no beginning, no end, no discernable shape, no perceptible distance in relation to the observer, no up or down, and it all feels like, "This is it! I'm seeing it." The recognition is cognizant of an emptiness that is also aware, and this empty awareness is perceived as being none other than your own. You feel in the moment that you are seeing your own mind in its natural state.

Few people ever get this far in even considering their own minds, let alone recognizing it is *right there*. You have just done it, have just recognized its innateness, and now the instructions tell you to rest in the view of it. And while you are totally relaxed, your awareness is very stable, there is something about the balance or 'tension' of this awareness that feels slightly off. You recognize mind, but the *ease* of resting in the recognition has not quite arrived.

It is here that you can return to your shamatha training and begin tweaking, ever so slightly, your awareness in the moment. This is called 'deliberate mindfulness,' because while awareness is indeed present, there is still some effort in maintaining it or allowing it to spin out into effortlessness. In this instance, the 'effort' needed would be to loosen the tension of it. Deliberate mindfulness is a more active or conceptually involved version of 'effortless mindfulness,' where the latter does not require any other effort beyond mere recognition and an easy resting in the natural state.

You might recall in shamatha training the tightening and loosening of one's focus on the rock, and the comparison was made to the tightening or loosening of a string on a guitar so the string could sonically settle on its namesake note. You do this here, tweaking the awareness around that imperceptible line you seem unable to cross – the line between recognition and resting. If awareness is too loose, you risk drifting around in lazy mind or nodding off into sleep or wafting around in a mindless haze where not even a thought has energy enough to arise in; too tight and, yes, things are clearly seen, but then resting in evenness is difficult to attain.

If you're noting this difficulty in a moment when resting is not so easy, then you can take-in a deep breath to fill the body and mind with refreshing oxygen. You can also slightly adjust your sitting position, loosen it a bit so that perhaps it releases some of the tension not only from the body but from the awareness itself. You can consciously pull back on your focus within the mind, making it a little more spacious so that perception becomes looser and somewhat larger, with greater breadth to its overall sweep. These are all little adjustments which can allow for that slight yet essential shift from recognition into an easy resting within our own essence.

But there is yet another shift which is critical to mind recognition, and going forward it will be the most important shift in perspective you do in your meditation. Thus far the pointing out has had us looking within in order to mindfully observe, but not just observe, *to recognize* that which is our eternal essence – this being none other than innate mind. Implicit in this is still a duality, in that the observer settles in and sees a mind that is not coming and going, has no up or down, nowhere from which it arises and no place to which it departs, and this we are told is our own naturally occurring mind.

Who, though, is doing this witnessing? Well, the first answer is likely to be, "Me! It is *I* doing the witnessing. *I* am the witness of my own mind." Here, your beloved guru would say, "Where is this 'I' that is doing the witnessing? Point to it. Touch it." We'll see later that this 'I' is nowhere to be found. It does not exist anywhere within the mind, and it is nowhere to be found in the actual body. Nor will one find a 'me' in the body or mind, and not a 'mine,' either. I'll elaborate on this in greater detail in later chapters, but even a quick scan here will lead to the finding of no 'I' doing the witnessing of mind in its natural state. So who or what is in witness? The answer is: mind is observing mind. Awareness is aware of itself. It sees itself and recognizes itself, and it is able to do this because the awareness that sees is none other than your own, and only you can be aware of your own awareness.

With the momentary evanescence of the 'I' there is a simultaneous knowing of an awareness that can *see itself* – the mind we recognize is the same mind doing the recognizing. This self-swallowing observance can have the impact of triggering an incremental shift within perception, one which eventually leads to a total tectonic shift in how we perceive ourself on a day-to-day basis. But in the moment we're feeling stuck, unable to arrive at an easy resting in the natural state, this small shift in perspective can cause the plates of perception to slip past one another, wherein tensions are at once released and we are now able to settle into an easy, effortless rest.

Recall the analogous guitar string being ever-so-gently tuned to its perfect note, or what might better be described as its naturally harmonic state. Here, the string gets cut. Between its two clipped ends there is now only emptiness. In that emptiness there is no longer a string, nor is there even the slightest anticipation of an awaited note. From the perspective of the string, we see it is now perfectly at rest, perfectly at ease, relaxed in doing absolutely nothing at all. Having been cut, there is nothing more for it to do, nothing more to create, no song in wait. All potential is released into emptiness. We are to be like this in our resting.

Prior to 'the cut,' our awareness may have been held in place from the 'I' doing the seeing, the recognizing. Now, a 'no-I' is in witness, which alone decimates the subject-object duality that otherwise is the modus operandi of conceptual mind. This one shift in perspective can allow for the sudden slotting-in to a resting that only moments before was so difficult to arrive at.

It is here where you see through direct perception the utter emptiness of your own natural state, and this emptiness is seen as a pristinely limpid openness, an immaculate oneness. You also see that this emptiness, this wide-open spacious awareness, is your very essence. You *are* the spaciousness and lucidity of it, the emptiness and clarity of it, and in this knowing you find yourself in perfect ease, perfect balance, in equipoise. This is the sweet spot we aim to arrive at in our meditation again and again, and it is exactly where the teachings tell us to rest. We do nothing more than rest when arriving here. Simply recognize and rest, rest and stabilize, rest and deepen and let insight, as it certainly will, receive the wisdoms which spring naturally and eternally from our awakened state.

Ouroboros

When looking at mind in its natural state, we look for *that which knows*. It is not an object we are looking for, not an other. Rather, mind looks at itself, sees itself, recognizes itself and then rests in this recognition. Mind sees mind, and in this reorienting view the subject-object duality momentarily dissolves. Awareness observes the emptiness of self, in that awareness sees not a self but *itself*, absent of an actual self. Any concept of an existent 'I' is obliterated in this moment of direct perception, and the realization of no self, no 'I,' is nothing short of a small awakening.

When first recognizing our own naturally occurring mind, the experience of it is typically short-lived. The shift back into conceptual thinking and the re-emergence of our embodying 'I' happens quite quickly. We lose connection to our awareness absent of an 'I,' and with it the awareness of an empty self is lost as well. This is entirely ok. We've been lifetimes and aeons not knowing our own minds, driven endlessly on winds of duality, so it will take some time to root ourselves in the new realization that the subject-object mindset is mistaken, a delusion borne-out wholesale by conceptual thought.

This is why we set ourselves to 'the practice,' where we meditate again and again in an effort to familiarize with the awakened state, when at some point we can fully inhabit what the masters refer to as buddha mind or our own buddha nature, the essence of which is in each of us.

Each time you are resting in realized awareness – the resting after recognizing mind in its natural state – you are at the heart of Dzogchen practice. You are not analyzing in this resting, or at least you are *mostly* not analyzing. Rather, you are observing, becoming familiar with and eventually becoming certain in the knowing that this is your mind you are resting in, not something unknowable or other-than.

This level of mind can only be rested in because, in its natural state, there is nothing about it that distracts, nothing within it that pulls us away from directly perceiving or inherently knowing. Only the conceptual mind distracts, and it does this by endlessly pulling us from presence. Innate mind cannot do this because it is presence itself, an empty awareness that is of no time, not even a present, since without thought there is no present. There is only the fourth time.

Look at space and you are seeing the emptiness of the fourth time. Couple this emptiness with awareness and there is now presence in the fourth time. Space is empty so it cannot pull, it cannot distract. It can only allow. It allows for anything and everything to arise. Without the emptiness of space, nothing can arise. There is nothing, not even the universe, that arises outside of space. So the emptiness is there. It is real. As an absence, it exists, and you can see it in the space in front of you, in the space that goes on and on throughout the infinite.

Similarly, mind is empty like space, and we see this when observing it in meditation. This emptiness is not what distracts, just as space does not distract when looking through it. The emptiness of it cannot pull us from awareness, since emptiness can only allow. It is an opening through which we see. Yet without awareness, even emptiness doesn't exist, since it would instead be a nothingness we would never even know about. The '-ness' in emptiness indicates its fullness. What is it full of? It is filled with our awareness.

Without awareness there is no presence in emptiness, and so there isn't even a fourth time. Being empty alone equates to nothing, an absence that is utter. With awareness, however, empty becomes full, and we as a presence in emptiness are now able to perceive. In our ability to perceive, however, we are also able to become distracted, though in our awakened, realized state we cannot.

Thought, the nature of which is awareness, arises in emptiness. In innate mind, a thought moves through awareness much as a bird wings through an open sky. The sky does not shake from the bird's movement through it. It does not follow the bird, which would imbalance both the bird and the sky itself. The sky, rather, allows for the bird to move through it, for that is its nature. Its nature allows. In our conceptual state, however, the natural occurrence of thought pulls us straight out of the fourth time and delivers us wholly imbalanced into the three times of past, present and future.

Our aim is to recognize the mind which exists in the fourth time, that which is empty yet aware. In recognizing it, we rest in its spaciousness, its openness, its *emptiness*, and in this we look to see the source of our recognition: *that which knows*. Who is the knower of this emptiness? Who or what is doing the knowing?

In mind training, it is this imperceptible zone between duality and non-duality where we allow our awareness to simply be – loose, easy, entirely at one within the emptiness. Here, without doing anything, awareness is allowed to totally rest. It is relaxed, unmoving, in absolute balance, spacious and wide open, and in this state of perfect equilibrium awareness is now able to slip beyond seeing the emptiness within itself – which is still a subject-object seeing – to perceiving the presence of itself. Awareness becomes aware of awareness, and in this there is an absorption. Subject-object seeing, in that ever-so slight perceptual shift, instantly vanishes and awareness and emptiness become immaculately one. Duality gives way to the natural state, wherein all appearances continue to arise but nothing is followed, nothing is attached to, nothing takes us from the essence of our self.

When entering mind in its natural state we recognize its emptiness, and the teachings then tell us to rest in the recognition. In other words, while resting we are still recognizing, or perhaps more accurately we are maintaining the recognition through a vivid, very stable awareness. Like a bell that's been struck, its sound sustains and resonates until it eventually dies out. There is no need to strike the bell again while the sound is sustaining. Once struck, we simply allow the sound to continue until it is eventually lost.

It is this way with our recognition. We recognize, and that is the striking of the bell, and then we leave it be and rest. We let that resting in empty awareness resonate until it dies out and distraction pulls us into another mode of perception. What is our recognition still recognizing after the initial strike? In observing the emptiness of all appearances, we very importantly observe the observer as well, and in our sustaining recognition we come to recognize the observer is none other than our own omniscient awareness. This recognition sees not the 'I' but an I-less awareness.

Who is the one recognizing mind? We observe this in a very open, objective manner. We let our awareness guide us in the finding, of seeing and recognizing. We don't let our intellect stand up and point out the obvious, which for the intellect would be the 'I' of conceptual mind doing the observing. If the intellect does step in and state what is obvious to it, then in this moment you are no longer in recognition mode; you are now squarely in conceptual mode. The sustaining sound of the bell has faded, died off, and it is time to re-strike.

While in recognition mode, you have the innate ability of being *insightful*, which is very different than being conceptual or perceiving conceptually. Insight within our settled awareness can inbreathe knowledge by mere observation. It can mindfully muse on the question, "what is it that knows," or "who is the witness in this knowing," and it can do this while still resting in sustaining recognition. Insight, in fact, is part of the harmonics of our sustaining recognition. Insight can mindfully observe, "Ah! There is no 'I' doing this witnessing," and that knowing becomes a frequency within the recognition that gives the overall harmonics of our recognition more range.

Insight informs experience, which in and of itself is a recognition, and so it is a recognition within recognition which becomes a kind of harmonics of recognition. Awareness sees the emptiness of mind, and in this recognition awareness also sees that it is observing itself. It becomes aware of its own omniscience and inhabits the perspective totally.

This is why I say we are *mostly* not analyzing, because implicit in our recognition is this insight which comes in the resting. The resting, then, becomes an active absorption of knowing, which on the conceptual level would be seen as analysis but in the non-conceptual mode occurs as realization. There is a natural inquiry taking place within the sustaining recognition of mind which allows knowledge to enter our experience, like an airy breeze through an open window. It is not knowledge borne of intellect but an innate knowing that arrives through our own all-seeing, all-knowing awareness. It is 'innate' because, indeed, it is already within us, this knowing, and it rises naturally into our awareness when at rest in our own natural state.

We enter mind and recognize its essence, which is emptiness. Emptiness clears away any sense of an 'I,' for the 'I' cannot exist in the recognition of emptiness. We rest in this recognition of a mind that has no sense of an 'I,' no sense of 'me,' no thought of "*I* am seeing this." Awareness observes the absence of an 'I,' observes the presence of its all-seeing self, and in this the recognition rings on.

In no longer perceiving an 'I,' awareness cannot help but fill the absence *with itself*. It becomes aware of itself and immediately self-knows, self-sees. It can do this only because there is no I-concept getting in the way. Awareness likewise sees, in looking at itself, that there is no beginning and no end to itself, that it does not arise from anywhere and does not go anywhere. It is simply there as an ongoing presence, as an *is-ness,* a *suchness,* a *that which knows.*

The emptiness we observe through direct perception is the same emptiness we see in the very space that surrounds our body. Space is empty, and we see this without confusion or need for explanation. Mind, in this same way, is also empty, and this too is plainly seen while resting in the natural state. What 'sees' is our awareness, the nature of which fills the emptiness and is inseparable from it.

For most of us, however, awareness has strayed from its essence. It has become deluded and now believes it exists independent of the very space it is naturally one with. The delusion thus gives rise to an 'I,' which then births itself over and over into bodies of every shape and kind. These bodies, in deluded perception, appear as separate and distinct entities within the space they each exist in. And on it goes.

Our efforts as Dzogchen practitioners are to train in seeing through the absence of an 'I' and become familiar with this absence. 'Absence' in this context is a positive: an affirmation of our own inborn awareness which is ongoing and unending. It sees not through the entity of an 'I,' and so perception is unsullied and pure. The resting in this absence, and the knowing of it, in turn cuts through our attachment to the body, which then further allows us to see our own essence in the space of naturally occurring mind. In seeing our essence, we begin the essential return to an awareness eternally one with the timeless everlastings of space, and this we call awakened mind.

Objects of Our Gaze

Wind is a natural aid in our quest to recognize the empty essence of mind. When it arrives in your part of the world, particularly when it is loud and blustery beyond the walls of your room, take the time to sit, meditate, and let its gustings play-out across the landscape of your settled awareness.

Why wind? Wind is one of the few things we tend to not reify. In other words, we likely don't turn wind into something seemingly tangible or vividly representational in the space of our meditative mind, or at least not in the more pronounced way we perceive the sound of, say, a helicopter. With a helicopter, for instance, even though we are not actually seeing its fuselage and blades from where we sit in meditation, the sound of it rotoring through the sky tends to mandate a manifest image in our mind nonetheless. We see it mentally across the screen of mind even though we don't see it in actual sight. This is protocol for the conceptual mind, which routinely generates images of things heard without actually having been seen, while it will similarly and simultaneously formulate a perceptible language as well – either symbolic or in actual words – which we see visually through inner sight to both signify and speak to the object of our hearing.

So in hearing the helicopter, the image of it now floats through the sky of mind in synchronized measure with the actual helicopter flying through the sky above. As such, the real helicopter in the sky and the rendered one in mind become indistinguishably one, and this is so only because we do not think to make that important distinction, for it is the habit of conceptual mind to conflate the two.

We hear, through the silence of our meditative space, the faint onset of the helicopter's familiar rumblings: softly at first as it enters our perception, then more loudly as it steadily approaches, its sudden thundering above before the sound once again falls fainter and fainter as it passes along on its trajectory elsewhere. As this narrative unfolds – 'narrative,' in that we tend to weave everything into storylines – it is the normal process of habitual mind *to see* some semblance of the sonically perceived helicopter, wherein it becomes a representational proxy moving through the mental landscape. This replicant image, however, the one arising solely in the mind, is not *less than* but, rather, one-to-one, a co-equal subject in the helicopter narrative of our normal thinking mind, to the point where not only an image is created but the conception of purpose comes as well: military, media, traffic, surveillance, fire, rescue. We see in mind and think in mind, and the two go easily hand in hand.

It's important to note that this mental re-imaging is a problem in meditation because the mind's endless arisings distract us from seeing the essence of ourselves, which is empty like space despite all indicators to the contrary. But it is not only in our meditation where this is a problem, for it is one of the key problems with perceiving in general, and it is likely the very problem which has led so many of us to meditate in the first place. We sense our way of perceiving is somehow off, that something about it is not quite right, and we sense this because if our perceptions were reliably correct then our level of suffering would be greatly diminished. Yet we continue to suffer, and to a lesser or greater degree we experience hardship throughout the entirety of our lives. Time and again we encounter the displeasure of heartbreak, anger, anxiety, stress, sadness, frustration, confusion, depression, fear – all of which occur as the direct result of how we perceive. We meditate, then, to train the mind in loosening its constrictive focus on the *things* in our world and to recalibrate our perception so we instead see the emptiness of those things, of all things, including, most critically, the empty essence of ourselves.

Wind counters our normal way of perceiving an object in that it bypasses the default mode of reifying, of turning sound into an image-object of mind. Since wind is a presence without appearance, it can freely move through awareness without mind itself prompting a representational image of it. Few other things are as triggerless. For example, when we hear feet walking toward us from another room, we tend to see in our mind's eye a person in approach, and perhaps we also think, "here comes so-and-so with my tea," if that is the present expectation; or the padding of paws might elicit both the image of your dog and the thought, "Beatrice is on her way...," and with that thought the image of your dog syncs up with the actual dog as she enters the room to perhaps lie comfortably beside you and drift off. Whatever the context surrounding the sound of those feet, our minds summon forth a corresponding image which likely aligns with some line of thinking – and maybe even a feeling – to form a cohesive narrative, or a preview which foretells, either correctly or incorrectly, the actual arrival of the person or pet into the room. This is perception in the habitual mode of fundamentally misperceiving, because before events have fully played out we've already seen and predicted the outcome in our imagination.

This inner imaging is a natural form of sense-making, a mode of self-storytelling which helps us bring coherence and intelligence to the five individual senses (sound, sight, taste, touch, smell), which on their own do not conceive. In the instance above, our mental consciousness, the sixth consciousness, prepares us for the moment when the actual person or pet arrives at the doorway of our eye consciousness, where we then see with our actual eyes and begin again an entirely new line of inner imaging/thinking. This interminable and tireless way of engaging with our surroundings is what the great meditation masters call 'the workings of habitual mind,' 'the monkey mind,' or any of the countless other 'minds' which have us endlessly foretelling and recalling, predicting and reliving, and it is our job as meditators to put an end to it once and for all. We must settle the trickster mind, quiet it in order to see it clearly and unmistakably for what it relentlessly does. Only then can we awaken into the essence of ourselves and be free from its pernicious hold.

Wind, then, becomes an ally in this pursuit. Without the myriad relational activities that arise when perceiving most other objects appearing to our senses – as with footsteps, or a helicopter – wind is perceived by mind yet passes through it without stirring up much in the way of relational imagery or thought. It arrives in mind as both actor and action without prompting, internally, a corresponding arisal. As a result, our settled awareness is more likely to observe it without attaching to it, and this gives us the opportunity to witness its movement through the emptiness of our natural state. We observe it in meditation not from a conceptual perspective but from the perspective of meditative inquiry, where awareness trains in observing an object as it moves through the emptiness of mind itself, not beyond it, not outside of the body.

Next is a sample inquiry meditation, more properly known as 'insight meditation,' and it is a good example of what this kind of observational inquiry in meditation looks like. It is a more active meditation than our normal resting meditation, which has the practitioner recognizing the nature of mind and resting in that recognition. Here, the object of our inquiry will be the sound of wind, but you can use any object for this kind of meditation. In fact, the full range of our experiences can be looked at in the same way we look at wind in the following chapter.

The Sound of Wind

Insight meditation is not a thinking meditation. It is, rather, an observation of mind wherein the practitioner obtains a clarified sense of knowing through direct perception. What is discerned and what is derived in this kind of meditation occurs without the normal filters of thought, without the organizing, appraising measures of thinking mind, and so the experience is direct. It is a perceiving without thinking, and this direct perceiving panes into a knowing that is more all-seeing and far more illuminating than any mere understanding through intellect could allow. This is called 'penetrating insight.'

A similar kind of knowing occurs when, say, tasting an orange for the very first time. When eating the orange, the knowing of the taste is direct. It does not come through thought. It does not arrive as an idea. It arrives as a realization, since the knowing permeates the whole of our awareness. No longer are we in notional wonder of the taste of an orange because the knowing with the tasting is now one, they are inseparable, where not even a thought could divide the taste from the knowing, the experience from the awareness.

It is this kind of experiential knowing we aim to arrive at when looking at our own mind in meditation. We get there by training in direct perception: the direct perceiving of the essential nature of all things, which is none other than emptiness. In perceiving emptiness directly, we become certain that not just some things are empty but all, since the entirety of our experience arises in mind, and all in mind is empty.

With enough practice, conceptual mind begins to fray. It unravels and comes undone, and what unfolds in the opening, as a kind of flowering, is our wisdom mind, which knows the essence of all. The fragrance of this flowering is the confidence we develop in the knowing. Confidence leads to certainty, certainty leads to further transformation and fast upon is the certain arrival of full realization, an awakening.

In insight meditation we directly observe the objects of our perception while simultaneously examining the manner in which those objects are perceived. Here, the object will be the sound of wind.

Begin your meditation sitting inside, away from the wind. Rest in the traditional meditative pose, which has you sitting upright, legs crossed, hands either folded in your lap or resting on the knees. Let the mind relax. Let it settle, clarify, and allow the space within the body to lighten and expand. Bring your awareness forward so that it is fully and actively present. You are conscious of breathing but not focused on it. Your body sits upright in your awareness, and here it might be helpful to imagine your physical body actually sitting *within* the wide-open, wholly allowing space of your own awareness. See this space of awareness as being no different than the enormity of space itself – that stretchless expanse which holds all the stars and planets in the universe – and your body sits like one of these satellites in the vast expanse of your own awareness.

You are mindful of your awareness, which contains all objects within it, including your body, including the sound of wind. You observe the wind moving through this space of awareness, much like wind moves through a boundlessly open sky. You are also mindful that your body, too, sits within that same boundless awareness, so that wind, in truth, moves only through awareness and not beyond it.

Wind is to space as thought is to mind. There truly is little difference between the two, and with this exercise you'll begin to directly observe their similarities. If a thought arises within this space of awareness, observe it as loosely and as unattached as you would the lifting of a breeze in empty space. Whatever the thought may be, allow it to rise up and drift along as if it were a single leaf on a light and lilting breeze, and you merely take note of the thought as you would any leaf aloft on a breeze, without feeling even a fleeting need to follow it on its meanderings into the unseeable beyond. The training here is in remaining the objective observer while also remaining stable in the stillness of your awareness.

What typically breaks such stillness and closes the space of awareness is thought, for thought reliably pulls us into states of distraction. When distraction occurs, when thoughts arise, you need only remember. What are you remembering? Remember to return to awareness. A simple reminder brings you back into the openness of present-moment awareness.

The words 'remembering' and 'meditating' should be seen as synonymous, for in the act of meditating we are continually reminding ourselves to remain aware. Thoughts in meditation inevitably arise, thus giving way to distraction, and the mere reminder to return to awareness brings us forward, where we become instantly and presently aware.

Take particular note of this spacious awareness which at all times allows for anything to occur. Awareness provides space for the easy rise of thought, a perceiving of an itch, the noting of your breath, and it equally allows for the wild, outdoor whippings of the wind. All of this occurs in the impeccable stillness of your own crystalline awareness.

A key query here, and perhaps the most important question you'll ask yourself again and again throughout meditation practice, is: what is the source of this awareness? How, in other words, are you knowing of the sound of wind? What is it that hears? Who is it that knows? Where is the exact source of this knowing? This questioning is a little bit like mental gymnastics, where you turn your awareness in on itself to look for where this knowing occurs.

You hear the wind. Does the knowing of its sound happen at the skin of the ear, where sound enters the canal and, *bam!* right there is where knowing occurs? Rest your awareness on that exact opening to see if this is where the knowing of sound occurs. Or does this knowing happen after sound enters the ear, where it arrives as a soundwave in the brain? Is it there, after receiving transmissions from the ear, that the brain interprets it as the sound of wind? Lay your awareness on the point where the hearing, i.e., the *knowing*, of wind is happening. Don't so much think about this as try to observe it within awareness. Receive insight from quiet, perceptive witness rather than trusted logic.

Perhaps this knowing isn't even taking place in the body – not at the ear and not in the brain – but is happening beyond the body, beyond the walls and windows that separate you from the outside wind. Perhaps awareness already knows of the wind 'out there' prior to the sound entering the ear canal. Is this possible? Where, as you sit in meditation, are you hearing the point of contact between awareness and the sound of wind? Where in your mind's eye are you seeing this knowing occur? Search with the spotlight of your awareness for where knowing meets sound, where the sound of wind meets the point of perception, and attempt to conclude where the exact location occurs.

By aiming your awareness toward a point of contact, you begin to acquire insight into a rarely considered truth: that no such point of contact can be found. The knowing of sound does not take place at the ear, not in the brain, not beyond the body nor beyond any wall that separates the body from the source of sound. Rather, the only 'place' where the knowing of sound occurs is within awareness itself. Awareness is the singular source.

This is a radically different concept from the one our thinking mind puts forward day in and day out. "Look at that bird over there," and we point to it 'over there.' "Can you hear it's song? It's coming from up in those trees." Insight meditation trains us to see the bird and its song in a different location: not 'over there' or 'up there,' but the knowing of both occurs only in our awareness. We see the world through the lens of awareness, and this one awareness is the sole source of our entire experience. We don't know of the bird because we see it 'over there;' we know of it because it appears in our awareness. Without awareness, the bird disappears, for it no longer exists.

Only through our meditation can we arrive at this more profound sense of knowing. The thinking mind does not allow for awareness to perceive in this way, for this latter mind is trained to see through the eyes and hear through the ears and perceive of things prepositionally – as being 'in that,' 'over there,' 'elsewhere.' But in actuality, all of it occurs in the one space of our awareness. Only through our practice do we begin to see this, and what we find through direct perception is that things 'out there' are nothing other than appearances in mind, and as mere appearance there is nothing to become attached to or rail against, for it is only an appearance. Let the sound of wind confirm this truth for you. In listening to it in your meditation, observe its relationship to your awareness to see if similar insights come into view.

You hear wind, and while it is indisputably *there*, it is also, upon close analysis, conclusively nowhere to be found. Its sound is present. It appears in awareness. Its appearance in awareness means there is a knowing. If there is no knowing then there is no appearance. The two are inseparable, as are emptiness and awareness, space and cognizance. Appearances arise in emptiness and the knowing takes place in awareness. The appearance is empty because it can only be found in awareness; the knowing of the appearance *is* the awareness, and so emptiness and awareness are inseparably one. Together they are seen as being mind as it naturally occurs – mind in its natural state.

Who is doing the observing? Only our awareness. Seeing this is the aim of our practice. In looking for the exact place where appearance meets knowing, you'll find the meeting of the two occurs nowhere other than in your own observable awareness. Continue to examine this essential point until you are certain of it.

How, then, through the fabric of your awareness, does the sound of wind weave itself in, and where do these first weavings begin? Seek the very point where sound arises in awareness. The wind outside blows. Where in awareness does the sound arrive? How does it enter? As it remains in awareness, how is it remaining? Merely observe. Does the sound have a quality to it, a substance, a shape which gives it a sustainable, seemingly substantial presence? Or is its presence in your awareness merely an appearance?

We can't just say yes or no to any of these ideas. We must experience them essentially, see their essence and therein arrive at a knowing, an irrefutable truth, and we must do this again and again in our meditation until a certainty takes hold. Certainty is key. Merely acknowledging "yes" or "no" does not deliver us there. Rather, we arrive at a certainty in knowing through direct perception, which is the very act of observing through awareness without thinking about what we are observing.

We now deepen the level of inquiry by considering: is the appearance of sound – in this case the sound of wind – similar to and as evanescent as a mental image or a thought? Indeed, make this comparison. Bring forth a mental image to see how it is either similar to or different than the appearance of sound. It can be any thought, of, say, a raven perched upon a branch. The wind outside dances the branch beneath the raven, but the raven itself, aside from a few ruffling feathers, remains perfectly still upon it. Allow this image of a raven on a branch to bear itself aloft in the space of your mind. Observe how the raven sits in mind and see if your way of perceiving it differs from how you are perceiving, in this same moment, the sound of the wind. The two occupy the same space, do they not, with the perception of both taking place within awareness? Or is the image of the raven being perceived differently in mind than the sound of wind? If so, then examine how they differ. Do they, if the latter is occurring, arrive at your awareness from two different perceptive portals, so to speak? Observe, and try to arrive at a knowing based only on what the mind sees, not by what logic tells you.

Regarding these seemingly dual appearances – one being the mental image of the raven, the other the sound of wind – if there appears to be differing portals of arrival, then is one portal of perception 'inner' and the other portal 'outer'? Observe to see how each are moving through the space of your mind. Be an objective witness, and be open to any insights that may arrive without thinking about them. You are aiming for a knowing that arrives only through insight, not thought.

Perhaps you're finding, or it may be just a sense, that the image of the raven inhabits the space of mind in the same way the sound of wind does, that their appearances are not dual but singular, not different but somehow one in the space of your awareness, like sound and image in dream. Take your time to observe without letting thought-logic pull things apart in an effort to conclude. Rather, you are merely watching, and with objective, carefree observation you allow the two appearances to reveal their natures as they actually are, not how the conceptual mind tells you they are.

If they are distinct – that is, the image of the raven abides in the mind differently than the sound of wind – then that would make them each distinct from your awareness as well, making your awareness a third and separate entity in the triad. Examine this possibility in your meditation to see if this is true. If you find that either the raven or the sound of wind is independent of your awareness, is separate from it, then that would make all three wholly independent and therefore the observed two would be isolatable from awareness, for they would be separate and distinct entities. Examine carefully to see if this is so.

If, however, you cannot make the distinction in your awareness between either the raven or the sound of wind, then this gives rise to the other possibility: that there are not three – raven, sound, awareness – but one, and that one can only be awareness, which, like space, allows for an entire universe of phenomena to arise in it.

With continued inquiry in this way, and with the insight derived, we come to see that thought arrives in mind much the way sound arrives in mind, and this is no less true for sight, smell, taste and touch. So rather than pointing the mind directly at the tongue in taste or the finger upon touch, we aim it instead at the awareness which observes any one or all of our five senses: sight, sound, smell, taste, touch. For it is this sixth consciousness, our awareness, which observes, interprets, and makes sense of the five other senses of the body.

. . .

At times it's helpful to take small breaks in meditation, especially when involved in these kinds of inquiry meditations where there is much to process. A short break to stretch the legs and get a cup of tea, or perhaps it's just about laying back and resting the mind for a few moments to consider some of the insights you've arrived at. Take whatever time is needed, and when ready return to the sound of wind and the inquiry of its passing through perception.

You return to 'the view,' which through practice is learning to see an emptiness of mind that is one with awareness. The two, we will always find, are inseparable. Like space, our essence is empty. Yet in that emptiness is a knowing. The knowing is our nature. Mind is considered empty because nothing within it can ever be found. Where is the sound of wind? Where is the raven? They appear in awareness, yet their appearance is empty because in looking for them we find no actual thing, nothing inherent, only an appearance. But they are not nothing, either, since our awareness still perceives them. So emptiness is not a nothingness because coupled with emptiness is a knowing, and the unity of the two equate to an all-knowing, all-seeing mind, and this is quite something.

Consider this oneness of emptiness and awareness as you move back into the spaciousness of your own wholly aware mind, and then begin to listen once again for the sound of the wind. Observing through the spaciousness of empty mind, you see there is a knowing, and this knowing perceives the sound of wind. Note the couplet of that last idea. Awareness is aware of the knowing which simultaneously perceives the sound of wind.

Wind is present and it is simultaneously perceived. We can use this sound to offer a bit of context. In observing the open, entirely unobstructed space of your awareness, hear the wind and see in your mind's eye how this sound both highlights and defines the emptiness of it. Like a bat echolocating through a darkened cave, let the wind sound-out the dimensions of mind. The sound moves through emptiness, yet it is in constant contact with awareness, just as a bat moves through the empty space of a cave and is in constant contact with its walls through reflection of sound.

Hear the wind but aim your attention toward that which knows of its sound. What knows of the sound? It is none other than awareness. Without awareness there can be no sound, for where without awareness can sound exist? To be clear, and to restate, the awareness we are attempting to observe, and self-know, is more accurately referred to as 'mind in its natural state,' and it is this mind we must come to recognize again and again in our meditations. Once we recognize it, and whenever we recognize, we then rest in this recognition and continue to observe.

This latter point is an important one to be cognizant of as you go about this inquiry, and if insights arise, but particularly if an experience arises where you believe you are recognizing the natural mind – which is empty and aware: empty because it cannot be found and aware because even in not finding there is still a knowing – then take the moment to rest in the experience of this realization. Do not continue to examine. Just rest and observe, rest and become one with the realization without analyzing. Even if you're not 100% certain that this empty awareness is your own mind in its natural state – perhaps you are *pretty certain,* but not 100% – then still rest in this experience without doing anything more than that.

At some point a thought will arise and you'll find yourself distracted. Not a problem. Merely return to the inquiry practice, which is observing how wind moves through awareness, and then continue in this way until observance leads to recognition and in this recognition you again rest.

Noting the wind, and perceiving the space of awareness through which it moves, are you able in any way to separate the two? Can the sound of the wind, in the very moment you are hearing it, be extracted from the mind that perceives it? Can the two be isolated, one removed from the other? And what about a thought? Can the arisal of a thought be pulled out or separated from this same space of awareness?

Sound and thought. In the space of mind, how do they differ? Closely look, though while looking you should attach to neither. Let neither thought nor the sound of wind pull you from the present awareness in which they both arise. Be like the old man on a park bench who tosses seeds to pigeons. He observes their movement with a notable lightness, with levity. He sees their many individual forms yet attaches to none. He doesn't single out a pigeon, give it a name, think of its backstory or the future it might one day encounter. Rather, he sits, watches, occasionally chuckles, yet all the while allows the little birds to be just as they are. He leaves them free to mingle, move about, move on. We need to be like this in our own minds, observing while attaching to nothing.

And so we observe how a thought arises and how sound might similarly arise in the same space of our awareness. Are either of the two divisible within this space? Can they be seen as being independent from that which perceives? Merely observe. Do not think about their occurrences, which in and of itself requires a dualistic approach to experience. If we think about sound or think about thought then we are maintaining the very subject-object duality we are aiming to be free of. Conceptual mind has it so the subject 'I' thinks and the object 'sound' is thought about. We are not doing that here. We are observing, not considering, and in only observing we are able to more perfectly see what is actually going on. It is direct perception as opposed to perception processed through concepts. Insight rather than logic.

Like a scent in the air or pigment in water, how can either thought or sound be separated from our awareness? If you are finding they cannot be separated, that they are entirely one with your awareness, then does this not make the two appearances in your awareness, thought and sound, a single essence in that awareness? If you are seeing through direct perception that this is true, and you are certain of it, then you can say that both thought and sound are 'of one taste' with awareness, each being equal as an appearance and each being one with your awareness, inseparable from it, and it matters little whether one arises from within or one arrives from without. As an appearance in awareness their essence is one, and that essence is emptiness. The fact that two things can be seen as one in awareness only highlights the essential meaning of emptiness, for if the two appearances were not empty then they could not be 'of one taste,' nor could they inhabit the exact same space, per the laws of our physical world. In arriving at this kind of seeing, rest in whatever insights might come and remain with this for however long awareness lasts.

. . .

When ready, bring your mind back to the sound of wind and for a moment rest in the knowing of it. The sound, you could say, moves, while awareness remains still, unmoving, just like wind itself moves through space while space simply allows for the movement, for space does not move since it can only allow. Let the sound wash around in this space of awareness, splashing up against the walls of knowing, and observe again how this awareness is exactly like space, with the one difference being that your awareness knows: it is conscious.

Listening to the wind, is it possible to say there is any other place where this knowing of its sound occurs, other than in mind? Merely listen, while at the same time observe the sound as an appearance in your awareness. Prior to this practice of direct perception, it might have been said that the sound of wind arrived from 'out there,' and this would have implied the sound was entering from outside of ourselves, that it was taking place beyond the body, beyond the walls, and the ears were merely picking up on it.

In observing with direct perception, however, we cannot say the appearance of wind is occurring anywhere other than in our awareness. The recognition of this truth, the experiential knowing of it, must be affirmed again and again so that there isn't just an ephemeral understanding of it. Instead, you must arrive at a certainty, a deep sense of knowing that is both irrefutable and unshakable.

Arriving at this kind of knowing is an arrival into the wisdom mind. You cannot get here by thinking. You can only arrive at wisdom mind from seeing through insight, experiencing through direct perception, and upon this arrival there is a spontaneous knowing that is profoundly experiential.

Spontaneous knowing comes from spontaneous presence. You can see how this all ties back to our practice, which has us training in presence while also training in direct perception. Direct perception is the one way of arriving at the recognition of our naturally occurring mind, for this mind cannot be seen through any other lens. An open, unsullied awareness is the singular portal, and it is toward this opening our practice shifts the awakening eye.

The I Entity

Space defines who we are as much as it defines the totality of our existence. As a physical body, the corporeal self, we are more space than matter, infinitely more, though from the conceptual perspective this is a tough argument to sell. The truth is, the human body – your body – is 99.99% space, and that incredible, near-incomprehensible percentage holds constant for all matter throughout the world, including all forms of matter throughout the universe entire.

Consider that number for a moment: the body is 99.99% empty space. Look down at the body you are currently inhabiting and see, against all appearances, that the self you observe is in no way solid. It is, as we've been hearing all along, a near-totality of emptiness, with just a little bit of something to get your hands around: a meager 0.01% of what you see as being yourself is solid physical matter, the grand sum of which you call your body. The rest is nothingness. Near zero substance. An emptiness through and through.

It is this truth we should consider again and again in our meditation, because in confluence with this truth is the nature of consciousness, which is not bound in the physical body but is rather one with the emptiness that gives space to our body. The body is virtually a totality of space. Mind and space are one, wherein space is to emptiness as mind is to awareness. If mind is inseparable from the 99.99% space that makes up the body, then it can be said that the body exists within mind and not the other way around. We are a body of awareness, within which exists a micro-sum of flesh.

But *really!* How can those numbers be? This seemingly absurd ratio between emptiness and visible form comes across as being a bit exaggerated, if not entirely outrageous. Surely the numbers are incorrect. Yet quantum physics tells us the numbers are precisely accurate, and the knowledge of this spacial totality within the body should be evidence enough to affirm we are not our body but are *so much more* than our mere existence in the flesh.

To that end, yes, there is a lot going on in this magnificence of flesh. We spoke to some of its intricacies, and its vulnerabilities, in the discussion of how glyphosate detrimentally affects the body's myriad life-sustaining functions.

From the quantum perspective, we look at the organism through the lens of space and see, as composite form within that space, it is teeming with cells, some 100 trillion of them. Within each of those individual cells there is something of around 100 trillion atoms. The nucleus of a single atom is roughly 100,000 times smaller than the atom itself, and between the nucleus and the atom's surrounding shell there is virtually nothing but empty space. Remove that 10^5 space from within each of our atoms and the human body would virtually disappear, shrinking as it would to the size of a lowly particle of dust.

Viewing this from the other side of the quantum lens, we see there is so much space within each atom that if its proton were enlarged to a tiny grain of sand, the atom itself would have a diameter of around 150 feet. Below the level of the proton lies the Planck, but it can more accurately be stated that the proton is swimming in a teeming sea of Plancks, known as PSU's, or Planck Spherical Units.

The Planck is the foundation of all things, the very basis for the existence of the multiverse and the source for what is nominally called the Unified Field. The Planck ocean *is* the Unified Field, and it is the dynamic energy source for all in existence. The Planck, then, and its ocean of spherical units, is point zero for that which we call mind essence. And though not considered matter, which my understanding has matter beginning at the level of the proton, the Planck does have a calculable mass, including tremendous mass energy deriving from its endless spin.

Were it possible to enlarge a single Planck to another grain of sand, the proton would have a diameter so large – upwards of 25 trillion miles – it would extend from where you sit to the nearest star cluster in our galaxy, Alpha Centauri, some 4.3 light years away. This, proportionally, is a tremendous amount of space within each and every one of the 100 trillion atoms inside but a single cell in the human body. Multiply that space again by the 100 trillion cells that make up the human body and, well, what you have is an enormity of space within the body that still seems entirely outlandish, but the numbers bear out and are verified in the meticulously scrutinized equations of quantum physics.

Such an immensity of space can give rise to musings on how, exactly, consciousness is able to inhabit the body, what with all the emptiness the body contains, the sheer expanse of which would seem to negate any kind of hold on consciousness, and particularly disallow for the creation of an identity so seemingly solid that we readily attach an 'I' to it.

So much space within a single atom, with one trillion atoms in each cell and one trillion cells within the human body. Imagine the space. Truly put your imaginative eye to the expanse and ponder: where in all that space is there a 'me' to be found? Where in all that emptiness lands the designation of 'my self'?

If the space between the Planck and the proton is proportional to the distance between Earth and its nearest star system, then perhaps we can imagine, poetically at least, that our own star system might have a singular, self-recognizing identity as well, one which perceives of a distinct body from the grand cluster of planets and stars that shape it into perceptible form. It might further perceive of unique and individual 'others' when looking at similar star systems in this galaxy and beyond, and it could say to itself, "this is me and that is them." And why not? This is exactly what we do in this body, which is proportionally equivalent in its relationship to emptiness and form.

You have our solar system, imaginatively speaking, which is conscious and alive and sees itself as one body amongst the many, and those many – each with their own individual consciousness – make up what we from Earth see as being the Milky Way, home to some 400 billion stars. Perhaps the Milky Way, too, as an entity, perceives of itself as being a singular, self-aware *individual* much in the way we do with ourselves, who each within our own bodies contain a proportionally galactic amount of space.

If consciousness in its deluded state grabs on to clusters of matter and claims those clusters as its conceptual own, labeling the composite gatherings with the nominative 'I,' then couldn't the Milky Way, or any number of other galaxies and star systems throughout the universe, be doing the same? Considering the nature of ourselves – of how individual consciousness is able to remain rooted even within an immensity of so much bodily space – then it is entirely possible that our solar system, too, and the Milky Way it is within, has its own conscious identity.

If such were the case, and we were able to look up and see our galaxy behaving as if it were separate from the whole, acting as if it were a unique character with its own personal story to tell – "my mother spun away from me when I was a wee solar system, not yet a galaxy, and I've never forgiven her. But *I showed her* by acquiring all these billions of stars, and now look at me: king of the universe!" – we might feel some compassion for the poor soul that calls itself the Milky Way, King of the Universe, knowing how deluded it had become. It had strayed from its source, which we see is largely emptiness. We know as well, because again we see it, that our galaxy is in no way isolated from the whole but is inextricably one with it all.

This, I think, is the true source of compassion, when we recognize that 'the other' is not seeing the world correctly, nor themselves. Rather, their delusion lies in seeing themselves as being separate from the rest, isolated, entirely alone. The heart wells with compassion in seeing what they, the isolated 'other,' do not. Naturally, you only want to help, if only to say, "the way you are seeing yourself in relation to the world is not correct."

Your greatest, heartfelt desire would be to show them how things really are, and your most gracious, compassionate gift would be to enlighten this deluded other to its more authentic state, its true essence. You'd want to say, "No, man! Look at yourself. You are so much *more* than a galaxy. You are conscious. You are aware. You are not *just* the galaxy but, in all truth, you are the entirety of the universe and the source of it as well. You are not separate from but one with all that exists. I can show you how to see this if you're ready. There is a technique…"

This is the compassion mystics have been showing us since the beginning of time, and the technique they offer is the one we put into practice in our meditation. Why, then, can we not just hear the words from these great masters and effectively 'wake up'? Because of the countless lifetimes in which we've been deluded, lost for so long in conceptual mindscapes that our intrinsic habits now function like elaborate, well-operating mechanisms which are not so easily dismantled. You cannot just walk into a factory filled with automated machinery and say, "Be gone!" You must piece by piece begin disassembling every one of the tightly integrated and systematically connected parts. This takes time, and this is where the practice – with each meditation and each time you enter the natural state – separately and in succession begins disentangling and then wholly deconstructing the highly organized components of standard-operating mind.

Even in reading this one brief summation of the quantum ratios of our body, we still cannot see with our eyes what we in time will see in our mediation, though only if we regularly practice. Try it now with your own body. Look down to see not its seeming solidness but, rather, the preponderance of space it more accurately contains, which is vastly more space than what appears as flesh. It's likely not something you'll be able to do with your seeing eyes, but with training you'll be able to accomplish it through in-sight, through looking at, recognizing and then resting in the knowing of your own spaciously empty yet naturally cognizant mind.

What holds you together is an idea, and that idea has at its gravitational core the concept of an 'I.' This 'I' lays across the landscape of conceptual mind like a sheet upon a ghost. Its thin veil floats for lifetimes upon the mind, taking on different shapes and different names depending on the life, but it likewise morphs continually even during one lifetime, weaving-in different concepts of a self that are each seemingly individual and identifiable. Rarely, though, does this 'self' recognize that beneath the fabric of conceptual mind is something else entirely, something more timeless and magnificent, a boundless spaciousness whereby dropping the garment of the conceptual 'I' allows for its lightful emergence.

We must let the cloak of ourselves fall and forever be done with it. Yet how are we to do this? The answer, again, comes down to recognition. Recognize the nature of your own mind and it is truly only a matter of time. In recognizing this naturally occurring mind the 'I' is excised from the perceiving eye, and this very swiftly opens the space for wisdoms of every kind to enter.

This one shift in perspective is actually quite seismic, to the point of being radically life altering, and not in some future far off but in the present here-and-now, for the awareness of 'no I' gives onset to an immediate shift. From here, barring a total betrayal of enlightened principles, your journey toward enlightened mind is virtually assured.

Looking for the Self

We begin looking for the 'I' by trying to find its actual presence in the body. Search in your meditation for where, literally, the 'I' can be found anywhere within. Begin somewhat globally. Meaning, look to the entire body as the container for 'me.'

"When I say 'me,' where in this body can I find this 'me'?" This is the mindset you go in with, searching the entire body of perceptible self so that, part by part, your eye narrows directly-in on areas like the hand, the heart, the brain, the buttocks. Wherever you sense the 'I' might exist in the body, you look with inward awareness to see if it can be found.

We go into this exercise with the knowledge of our body being 99.99% space, so if there is any 'I' to be found it would exist in its manifest matter, which totals a mere 0.01% of the whole. And though that latter number indeed seems scant, our manifest form nonetheless has an appearance, and that appearance is the basis for our own highly personalized 'I.' Where in that appearance does the 'I' abide? With rigor, we look for it in our meditation.

When looking at your body, where amongst the whole do you feel the 'I' is strongest? Let's say we begin with the default answer, which for most people is, "I am my entire body." "*Where am I?* You're looking at me! This *is* me, all of it, from head to toe." If this were so, if the self could be found in the totality of the body, then it follows that this same self, denoted by an 'I,' can be found in the body's various parts: in the hand, for instance. Look at your hand, doing so not with the habitual eye but with the analytical one.

From the wrist outward to the tips of your fingers, is there a 'me' to be found anywhere in that hand? In other words, can you lay your conceptual 'I' on that hand and say, "Yes, *I* can be found in that hand. I find the actual 'I' of my self right there in the hand, and I can touch it with the finger of my other hand." Is this the experience you have in looking for the 'I' in the hand? "Yes," you might say upon first glance. "I see an 'I' in that hand just as clearly as I sense a very solid and present 'I' in the whole of my body."

If this is your sense of it, then begin by looking at the hand for what actually is present beneath the designation. We call it a 'hand,' and so we look at the shape of the hand to find an actual hand beneath the designation of it. Naturally, we are looking for the 'I' in the hand as well, but first we must confirm there is even a hand there before we can look for the 'I,' which may or may not be one-to-one with the hand.

In looking for this hand, however, beneath the designation 'hand' we find there is no actual hand, because 'hand' is more concept than thing. The actual 'thing,' in fact, is nonexistent. The label belies the inherence of form.

How do we arrive at this conclusion? When one begins looking closely at the hand, it is seen quite readily that no hand inherently exists beneath the label 'hand.' We see this by laying a more critical eye on the skin sheathing the so-called hand. The skin is not the hand, for it is only skin, and we call it such. This skin covers the fingers which themselves are attached to the so-called hand, yet the fingers are not the hand, either. They are called fingers.

If we were to remove one finger, we would see in looking at the finger that no actual finger is there, either, for the finger itself is made up of individual bones called phalanges, and there are three of these per finger. We also say there is a knuckle on the finger, but the knuckle is not the finger. Instead, the knuckle is referred to as a joint. Still, pull any of those phalanges apart at the joints and it would be difficult to say there was ever a finger there in the first place, let alone joints, for there is no joint without the attendant bones... And so on.

This kind of analysis would continue, if necessary, throughout the construct of the entire hand, where we could look through all of its many individually named muscles and into the 100 or so different ligaments and tendons, its blood vessels and nerves – all of these in composite we call the hand but none of them individually are the hand.

This, as you can see, makes it very difficult to find an 'I' in the hand when the hand itself does not exist beneath its designation. With direct analysis you find in the positive sense that there is no 'me,' nor is there an 'I' to be found anywhere in the hand, because not even a hand can be found in what we call 'the hand.'

This one analysis alone should call into question any assumption that an existent 'I' can be found within the body, and "you're looking at it," because if the body were solid enough to hold the designation of an 'I,' then every part of that body would need to be equally in hold of the same designation. We feel our 'I,' perceive it to be within ourselves and thus say "I am." Yet where is this 'I' in our actual self? Where in the body can we find it? Our search here very clearly turns up no 'I' in the hand, because not even a hand can be found there.

But we don't stop with the hand, because our sense of our own present 'I' is strong – too strong, in fact, to be called into question by any close inspection of a hand. But to make sure the 'I' doesn't sneak itself back into the one 'hand' just scrutinized, we cut off the hand in our meditative mind and lay it in front of us. Again, this is an exercise of mind, and we are not actually chopping off the hand. We cut the hand off in our mind and we place it in front of the sitting body. We then look, mentally speaking, at the hand as it lies before the body to see if the 'I' might still somehow be in there. And though perhaps we still see it as some semblance of a hand, severed as it may be, we can affirm that the hand on the ground in front of us no longer represents 'me' because the basis for that 'me' is no longer present: it now lies as discarded matter on the ground.

For good measure, again in your meditation mind, you cut off the other hand and toss it in with the first, because conclusions arrived at through one hand will undoubtedly be the same conclusions arrived at with the other, and you don't want that remaining hand to lull you into thinking it might still contain an 'I' or convey any false sense of 'me.' That is, of course, unless you're still feeling attached to that one remaining hand. Perhaps you're still feeling the attached hand is one with the identifiable self, one with 'me' and therein one with the wholeness of 'my body' – "I am *in* this body, including my hand." If so, then analyze the still attached hand in the same way you looked at the now discarded one, and when ready – that is, when you see there is no 'I' to be found in that second hand, nor an actual hand beneath the designation – cut it off and toss it in with the first.

If you're symmetrically minded, then you now look at the feet to see if you can find an 'I' in either of them, and proceed in your analysis in the same manner as with the hands. Again, you would look at the foot, either the left or the right, and try to see where an actual 'I' or 'me' or 'mine' might be found in or on or around that foot. Find in the foot anything that conveys a 'you.' Look at the foot as a whole, and if you can see an 'I' there, then point your mind directly at the spot and see what appears. If an 'I' does exist there, then you should be able to reach out and touch it, just as surely as you can touch the foot itself, for the 'foot' and the 'I' should be a unit. The designations will be interchangeable if an 'I' truly exists in the body.

Yet no matter where the eye lands on the foot, it will likely not land on anything that communicates the entity of an 'I,' nor will it communicate the actuality of a foot, for what the eye first lands on, much as with the hand, is the skin of the foot. The skin, as we saw with the hand, is not the foot since we call it 'skin.' In peeling back this mere covering of the foot, and wherever we lay our searching eye beneath, one finds muscle and blood and again we find bone. None of these are the foot, for they are only the many elements that make up what we call a foot.

But if we were to look for 'foot' in any of those parts, we might get lost in the numbers, since we'll find there are nearly 30 individually named muscles, nearly the same amount of individually named bones, a similar number of joints, many dozens of tendons and ligaments, yet none of these individually or collected together can be called an inherent foot. The same can be said with the toe, which like the finger is but a collection of bones, joints, muscles, tendons, veins, etc. In none of this will we ever find the global 'I' we say is one with the whole, for even in the universally agreed upon designation of 'foot,' no foot can be found.

When no 'I' and no 'foot' are found in either of the two feet, we mentally cut them off and toss the two feet in with the two hands to create a growing pile of empty parts, 'empty' in that not even their given designations are applicable to the parts. With that, you look down on yourself and see that you still have a body with two arms, two legs, a torso and a head. You see that 'you' are still relatively whole, and thus the analysis continues.

Obviously, you can look down at one of your legs and continue the search for the actual leg in the designated 'leg,' wherein you'll find, not unexpectedly, not a leg but a large collection of individually named parts: a large swath of skin – which in and of itself is not singular, not a oneness but a multiplicity of cells that amount to the epidermis, the dermis, the hypodermis; there are sweat glands in the skin, hair follicles, blood vessels and fat and connective tissue.

Beneath the so-called skin, there are numerous powerful muscles in what we call a leg. There are also three large, individually named bones: the femur, the tibia, the fibula, none of which can be called 'the leg' for they are only components of. There is another bone in the leg called the patella, or kneecap, which is clearly not the leg but is also clearly no basis for the perceived 'I,' either. And if you imaginatively choose to crush up those bones and combine the powders into a heaping pile, then toss in the ground up muscle and veins, tendons and nerves – all of which make up the nominal 'leg' – you would no doubt concur there is no leg to be found in the recombined sum of its parts, nor, likely, will you find any basis for an 'I.'

So rather than doing all that messy unpacking of the leg, perhaps you cut it straight off in the meditative mind and hold it out in front of you. Begin scouring it with the analytical eye in an effort to find, "where in that leg was my 'I'?" The clear and obvious answer is that the 'I' was never there, that the leg, like the hands and feet, could not possibly be in hold of any actuality of an 'I' because they themselves are not the actual things we've labeled them to be. Inherently, a leg is not a leg, a foot is not a foot, a hand is not a hand. Their designations are purely conceptual, mere concepts borne of composite form.

You look down on a body that remains and perhaps find comfort in knowing the 'I' must still be one with what is left, because even though you've cut off a leg, two hands and two feet, you still feel a strong sense of an 'I' in the body that, admittedly, is less whole than when the analysis began. And with that you bid the leg adieu, drop it in with the severed hands and feet and continue on in your analysis with the other leg, then the two still attached arms – the three of which you'll find, again in the positive sense, that no definitive self can be found in any of the body's extremities.

For clarification purposes, in saying "the positive sense" of not finding yourself in these parts, you are acknowledging two things: one is that you positively do not find a basis for the designating 'I' in the limbs that were just analyzed, so with continued analysis in this way you can conclude and become confident in the fact that 'you,' under close inspection, cannot be found in either of your two hands, two feet, two arms or two legs.

The other 'positive' here is that if *you* were to be found in any of those parts, this would mean trouble for your long-term self: the soul, or the ongoing consciousness, the karmic being, enlightened mind, the higher self or whatever it is you're aiming to understand in this lifetime. For if *you* were inherently bound to any of those parts, and by extrapolation the whole of the body – for the body is not a body without its individual parts – then there would be no hope for awakening beyond them. If you were your knuckle, for instance, then you could not be anything other than that knuckle, ever, not even in death. And if that knuckle were ever to be accidentally severed from the body – say in some freak accident you lose your pinky finger – then a section of *you* would be removed from your eternal self in the actual and permanent sense. Worst still, when the whole of your body does eventually die, as it is destined to do, the whole of *you* would also die with that body, and that would be that. *Kaput!* The existence of you would end there and then. So this exercise is intended to bring comfort, and confidence, to the truth that you are so much more than the body, and the analysis of seeking the self within the parts is one that eventually brings certainty to this fact.

Now your analysis going forward need not be so grisly or surgically comprehensive as it has been in the examination of the hands and feet, since, indeed, you saw how neither *you* nor any basis for the designating 'I' could be found in the skin, muscles, veins, ligaments, tendons, bones or joints of either the hand or the foot. Yet at the same time, you are not to so speedily move beyond further analysis on grounds of it perhaps feeling repetitive or overstating the obvious. If the obvious were so obvious, and if attachment to the body weren't so strong, then the need to look for the attendant 'I,' i.e., an actual self within the body, would not be necessary. So you'll need to find a balance that is right for you in this particular meditation.

If your own sense of an 'I' is intimately and inextricably bound with your body, then you might need to go further into detailed analysis when searching for this sense of an 'I' in every single part of the body, taking each limb down from skin to bone to beyond even bone, where even the cells and atoms of those constituent parts are isolated and closely inspected in the meditative mind, searching all the while for any basis of an 'I,' 'me,' 'mine' – 'my leg' or 'my hand.' Also, if you're finding it painful or particularly gruesome to remove in your mind any part of your body, then all the more reason why this meditation is important for you to perform, since this means attachment to the body is especially strong and your sense of an 'I' is deeply entwined within all of it, so a comprehensive search would be beneficial.

Also, there is another element to this practice that might be helpful to some, but especially for those who are already practitioners of the Eastern or shamanic traditions, and that is you can ritualize every detail of this practice – known in certain lineages as chöd practice – by visually offering your bones and viscera to the gods, to Buddha himself, to any single entity you might hold dear or to an entire retinue of enlightened beings who symbolically might appreciate an offering of your imagined self.

To do this, once you have your detached limbs lying before you, you take the time to strip each leg and arm down to the bone. You would then take four of the largest bones and lay them crosswise to create a stand which will eventually hold a skull. The setup looks like a rudimentary cooking-system over a campfire, that iconic iron one we see in Westerns where four iron rods support a pot above a fire. In this case, the iron rods are switched-out with four long bones from the extremities, and rather than the old iron pot the crown of the skull is used instead, which will ultimately hold all the parts of the body that were stripped clean, thoroughly examined, and tossed into the skullcap after having found no basis for the attendant 'I.'

The chöd practice is an extraordinarily powerful one. It is a foundational practice in the Tibetan Bön tradition and is regularly practiced across the many lineages of Tibetan Buddhism, most notably in the Nyingma and Kagyu schools of Tibet. The great Tibetan master Namkhai Norbu Rinpoche, one of my fierce early teachers and a renowned chöd practitioner, said in his book *The Crystal and the Way of Light*, "[Chöd] is a practice in which one works to overcome attachment and ego-clinging by making a mentally visualized offering of one's own physical body." He continues:

> The practice is principally undertaken in lonely and desolate places, such as caves and mountain peaks, but in particular graveyards and charnel grounds at night, when the terrifying energy of such places serves to intensify the sensation of the practitioner who, seated alone in the dark, summons all those to whom he owes a karmic debt to come and receive payment in the form of

the offering of his body. Among the invited are Buddhas and illuminated beings, for whom the practitioner mentally transforms the offering into nectar, and all the beings of the six realms, for whom the offering is multiplied and transformed into whatever will be of most benefit and most pleasing, but also summoned are demons and evil spirits to whom the body itself is offered as a feast just as it is.

Rinpoche concludes in saying, "By summoning up what is most dreaded, and openly offering what we usually most want to protect, the chöd works to cut us out of the double bind of the ego and attachment to the body. In fact the name chöd means 'to cut'; but it is the attachment, not the body itself, that is the problem to cut through." [p. 47-49]

It must be noted that the elements of chöd being discussed here are greatly distilled and merely introductory, and the practice in this book is further merged with another practice, a Madhyamaka insight meditation, which aims to realize emptiness through this kind of close analysis of designations, but the two are entirely complimentary and nicely work hand-in-hand.

We continue with our search for the 'I' in the body. How is it being perceived, this 'I,' 'me,' 'myself,' 'mine,' in relation to the body you currently occupy. Where, precisely, do all these implicities land in this body? We say 'my body,' but who is the 'I' this body belongs to?

It was seen through direct analysis that an 'I' cannot be found in the extremities. What remains for our search is the torso and the head, and it is in this region where most of us sense the 'I' is strongest, so surely it would be here if it exists at all. If an 'I' does exist, then through exacting analysis it can surely be found.

Sitting comfortably in your meditation space, breathe in through the torso and allow the breath to fully expand, and let it rise and cleanse as it moves up through your head. Then release, and with it release any attachment to the body you might still feel. Observe your body as an object of insight and nothing more. It, the body, is not you, though it is through this analysis you will come to recognize this essential point. There are many ways of going about this mental exercise, and one way can be in imagining a knife slicing open your chest, and piece by piece you begin to pull out the organs in search for which organ in particular might be ground zero for the 'I.'

Or perhaps instinct pulls you straight to the heart. If you're feeling the heart is the source of your perceived self, then take the time to piece it apart, chamber by chamber, sorting through the ventricles and veins, the valves and things such as the pulmonary trunk, the ascending aorta, the superior vena cava, the auricle of left atrium – to name but a few elements of the heart – and see if in any of those labels or organic bits hold the source for your own sense of an 'I.' When it cannot be found, let the heart fall into the pile of discarded parts in front of you.

A good portion of your body is now in pieces, severed from the whole, and perhaps here we cut straight to the chase and remove the head from the torso, for the head is typically perceived as being the conceptual container for our 'I,' and surely the last remaining outpost where it can possibly be found.

You take off the head and give it a close inspection. You look upon its face and see, indeed, that it is your face, the one you recognize from seeing in the mirror each day. Can the 'I' be found in that face and, if so, where in its countenance do you find it exactly? Or perhaps you sense the 'I' is not so much within the face but beneath it, one with the brain. Slice off the crown of the skull just above the eyes and ears so that the brain is now exposed, and place the skullcap on the cross-sticking of bones that perhaps you've already set up for an offering. Imagine the skullcap expanding so it is large enough to hold all of your body parts.

Your brain is now exposed, yet your awareness is drawn to the eyes, which are open and staring back at you. The eyes, you observe, connect directly to the brain, so perhaps you're able to find the 'I' in those windows to the soul. Remove the eyes, your eyes, and see if you can find an 'I' in either one of them. Is the eye even an eye, and if it isn't, how could it possibly window the so-called soul of self? Look closely. We call it an eye, but is it an eye without its sclera, the cornea, the anterior chamber? Remove those from the surface of the eyeball, and then search deeper for the designating 'I,' or search for the actual window into the soul by removing the iris and pupil, together considered the eye's lens. Each are key components to an eye, but they are not the eye proper, for already in removing those six elements to the 'eye' we see, again, that an actual eye beneath the designation doesn't exist, at least not intrinsically. Rather, like everything else in the body, the eye is a composite of individual parts, with each of those parts not inherently being what they're called. You cannot say the lens of an eye *is* a lens, either, because the lens, too, can be further dissected to the point where there is no lens but a collection of cells, and the cells are even further anatomized to find, in the end, mere atoms and a preponderance of space. Where, then, does one find 'me' in all of this? Where *am I* in any part of this body *I am in*?

When looking closely at the body, or anything else for that matter, we find beyond the labels that, in the end, there is no *there* there.

It is at this point, after an exceptionally thorough examination of the body total, we can conclude there simply is no 'I' to be found in any of it. You cannot now say "I am" with reference to the body and still believe there is something of inherent existence to be found. Rather, what we find is but a concept. The 'I' is conceptual, not actual.

Thus, you bring an end to this rigorous investigation by offering up all the parts of your body in whichever way it feels appropriate: as nectar to the enlightened beings, as remittance on a karmic debt, as benefaction to those in desperate need throughout the six realms, or as feast for the demons and evil spirits who might each be appeased by your gracious offering.

Still, the question remains: how is it that *I am*? What is it that holds my awareness? The answer, we are finding, can only be space. The fleshly body has a gravity which holds awareness in place, yet the body of our awareness is the emptiness of space.

Ghost Stories

In looking for the 'I' and not finding it anywhere in the body, we now look for that which defines us, the labels we place on ourselves and the stories we tell that both engender and ossify our otherwise fluid identities. These stories add flesh to the embodied self, yet in themselves they are all but tales of constructed mind, concoctions of memory, anecdotal revenants from the dead days of an ongoing life. They are trickster entities, these tales, that offer up personhood and persona and provide for a distinguishable 'I' where no 'I' inherently exists. More problematic still is how invested we become in these fables of self, believing down to the detail the sum of which we ourselves have so craftily stitched from a lifetime of seemingly relatable events.

To this point we've looked for an 'I' and found only its absence, and so we continue to close the circle by looking at the phrases that speak to an existent self. In doing this, we can expect these designations, too, will not be found. And though we expect this, we must nevertheless look because our *I*'s and *I am*'s are full-bodied within us, both as psychic entities and as fleshed-out ideas.

An easy one to begin with is the nationality self, that dutiful "I-am-the-country-I-live-in" personage. "I am American," taking myself as an example, is the kind of blanket designation which wraps us warmly in its bolstering cloth, offering us an aspect of identity that is as much collective as it is personal. For many, this one label is a conception of self that is nearly impossible to shake because with it comes a certain pride in owning the designation as birthright, then wearing it as an ennobling cloak. Time and again we see how deeply problematic this attachment can be, for at its worst it rousingly stokes the flames of unaccountable, unanswerable identity to a ruinous pyre.

As individuals we become particularly wedded to the concept of nationality – "one nation under God" sums up the romance of it quite nicely – for in it we allow ourselves to merge with the motherland and feel united and protected under the nation's prevailing, unfailing God. So attached as individuals to this national identity that we are easily won over to the worst of its tendencies, culminating most lamentably in outright war with other designations – other citizens, that is, from nations who don't so easily or amenably align with our own upright designation. In doing this, in acting against others in an effort to defend or further spread our national identity, we cinch tighter the noose-like cord that ties us to the collective, defining us even more strictly and solidly in terms of who we think we are both as a nation and as citizens of the land.

Yet defining oneself through nationality is an obvious red herring, as far as stories go, and it is one of any number of false flags we stake in ourselves that can easily lead to all sorts of inappropriate behaviors: any number of aggressions and heavy-handed actions that might not otherwise occur were not the concept itself so freighted, so infectiously charged, and so communicable. Which leads us to ask, as we did with the 'I,' where is the 'American' within the self? Like the 'I,' we look for the concept in our actual body, and in not finding it we have the opportunity to release this one big fish into the cleansing waters of our wisdom practice, wherein we focus on those quieter designations of perceived self which are far more slippery and difficult to catch.

Less easily recognized, though powerfully configuring nonetheless, are tales told about us and to us – short, swift summations which from one person might have us as being, say, callous or even cruel, while from another we might be seen as the nicest person they've ever met. These descriptions, too, find throughways into our perception of self, trickle deep into the subsoils of who we consider ourselves to be and, if heard often or emphatically enough, begin to germinate. Naturally, such descriptions running counter to our own preferred storylines – of being callous and cruel, for instance – are promptly relegated to the narrative crypts of our shadowed withins, there but to haunt and on occasion lift into the spectral fabric of this day's tale or tomorrow's telling, each its own phantom in vie for an in.

"I am an angry person," he tells me. "I am always afraid," you tell yourself. "I am depressed." "I am gay." "I'm an addict." As we begin to observe the labels we place on ourselves – these, mere chapter headings for our own personal stories – we begin to look for where these designations lie within us. Whatever is said, and whatever you tend to say about yourself, look for where that designation lands inside the body.

Where is the 'addict' in this body of yours? Where is the 'I' and where is the 'addict'? No need here to look for the 'I' as we did in the previous exercise – in the hand, the chest, the brain – or even to look for the 'addict' in these same areas, for we know the finding. That being said, you can and should do the 'looking for the I' exercise many times until the certainty of 'no I' truly enters the weavings of who you see yourself to be.

Here, we are looking for the attaching designations to that 'I,' and to illustrate this idea we'll hold closely to the 'addict' designation as but one example of how you can use this technique for all other designations: depression, debilitating fear, anxiety, shyness. All of these so-called conditions can be looked at in the moment we're experiencing them, and we find again and again in the light of our dispelling gaze that they promptly disappear, at least in the moments we are looking. Which is why we call this 'a practice,' because you do this 'looking' over and over until you obtain some level of power over these designations, these seeming conditions, so that somewhere down the line you learn to master what till now has so handily mastered you. It is a powerful and even transformative practice, one in the arsenal of an entire body of practices we use to arrive at recognizing of our own innate minds, which cannot be seen with our stories in the foreground.

If, to employ the example, you've already acknowledged that you have addictive tendencies, and there is proof in the trail of trouble those tendencies have wrought, then the compact designation of 'addict' locks right into your sense of an 'I,' which is likely deeply rooted in the concept of yourself. Yet in the same way the 'I' vanishes in the space of our clarifying awareness, the attaching designations to that 'I' similarly lose all power to define when the eye of mind is directly on them.

"I am an addict," you say with confidence. "Yes, I can vouch for this: he is definitely an addict," say others. The concept has been sanctioned by not only yourself but by the community at large, and so it lives. But where in the body does it live? Where can the actual addict be found?

In the nominative mode, 'addict' in this context refers to a person or a thing, i.e., something that actually exists. Is 'addict' a person or thing? In the manner it is being conferred here it is unquestionably a person. It is perceived as 'person' and accepted as *the* person because this is how it is communicated through our language.

Language, in that sense, is indeed communicable. It is infectious, and in receiving the infection of language, to extend on William S. Burroughs' observation of the word, it spreads like a virus throughout the whole of ourselves until there is no distinguishing between the 'I' and the 'addict.' The two become expeditiously one the moment we put language to it. So what is the corrective?

We palliate the word with our one-pointed awareness, and through observation alone we remedy the infection. This becomes a near-surgical procedure in that our needle-like gaze is laid directly on the disturbance, and in this we examine.

Not Finding, Forgiving

To begin looking for the 'addict' within ourselves, we first do a quick scan of the body to look for the 'I,' which we know will not be found. If you are still unsure, then continue to look for that 'I' until you are certain it is not there. Arrive at a knowing, via direct looking, that the 'I' of your body does not exist.

In this insight meditation, however, what we are really looking for is the 'addict,' of which the 'I' designates *you are*. Yet it need not be only the 'addict' where we employ this dispelling technique. It can be any and all of the other designations we self-attach in order to define our experience, be it depression (as in "I am depressed"), anger, the litany of phobias – the lot. Here we are using the example 'addict,' where it, like the 'I,' will nowhere be found. Still, we can't just say, nor can we infer, that the addict doesn't exist. We must look for the truth of nonexistence, for the absence of an entity borne exclusively of concept.

"I am an addict" is an idea, the very notion of which has been offered up, accepted, and summarily attached to your present sense of self. 'Addict' comes coupled with your singular 'I' and together they erroneously sum up an aspect of who you are, your character, of that which is agreed upon and sanctioned by the community, the family, the dearest of friends.

Now this is not to say you still don't have addictive tendencies, or that these same tendencies aren't causing notable problems. The discussion here is not whether to acknowledge or negate an existing condition and the consequences arising from this condition. Rather, the discussion at hand is aimed directly at the philosophical and spiritual practice of looking fearlessly at the labels that define us, be they this one or any of the other designations which, if affirmed often enough, become a sort of living, breathing entity with your name squarely on it, your name and the coupling label totaling a singular One.

Again and again we look for the addict within the landscape of the body, and time and again we do not find it, and we continue this looking until the drag of that label begins to lighten, its tentacles one by one begin to loosen and unstick.

Still, even when we become certain the label is not inherently our own – it does not define us and wants not to lift us – there are nevertheless the pressing and persistent impulses which are impossible to ignore, and they should not be ignored. In fact, quite the opposite is demanded of us, and it is their total attention that shall be given. Say, for instance, the addiction is to alcohol, and you recognize the many moments when the craving to have a drink is strong. The impulse feels deep within the body. Surely, upon scant consideration, it must arise from somewhere within because its encroachment through mind and its pervasiveness in thought feels far too pronounced to be solely projected from mind's fainter breathings.

When such impulses arise and the cravings are strong, we don't act, we merely look. From where in the body does the impulse arise? Having looked for the 'addict' and not found it, we now look to find the craving itself. "Where in my body does this craving feel the strongest?" This is a calm observance, one where perhaps you momentarily sit with a cup of tea and relax into it, if this is at all possible. But standing up wherever you are when the craving locks in is perfectly doable as well.

Let your awareness turn inward and do a meticulous scan. Observe the area of the tongue, where perhaps in this moment the signals to have a drink are being conveyed most pressingly. The tongue nearly laps at that which is not there. The throat contracts, swallows. Awareness looks around the tongue, and when you see the craving does not rest there, is not even occurring there, you then mindfully move down the throat and observe again for wherever the craving rears its disquieting head.

Again, this is not lazy looking. You are looking with absolute diligence and with the sincere intention of finding the exact location whenever an impulse arises. "I need a drink." Where is this *need* arising in the body? Where are you feeling it? Perhaps it isn't the tongue specifically, but maybe it's somewhere in the mouth. Look with your mind's eye directly in the mouth, at the mouth, around the mouth. From wherever internally you're experiencing the craving, look to where the experience has a center and wait for its reveal. You'll find it moves, and wherever your awareness lands it will not be there, even though it seemingly just was.

This targeting with the mind, in fact, causes not just our cravings but all things, all designations, all impulses to fall deep into hiding, to even disappear, and it is only through our one-pointed awareness that this can occur. We circle-in hawk-like, searching, laying our taloned gaze on that which ultimately will not come into sight, for in the looking we see it has no inherent existence.

The technique, by the way, works with everything. Anything we experience, just turn the eye inward and look for the source. It works, as said, at dispelling anger, anxiety, depression, even hiccups can be interrupted when the mind's eye is laid directly on their point of arisal, for in the looking the site seemingly vanishes.

The fact we do not find these points of arisal in the body means the experience of addiction or anxiety, anger or even pain is not taking place in the body. Rather, everything we experience occurs exclusively in mind. Even our search for all said conditions takes place in mind, for the search itself is a scan through the mental body, the body we see in mind.

Pain, it must be acknowledged, is much more difficult to work with, but pain, too, can be brought into this practice with impressive results. An example of the power of this practice comes, regrettably, from an experience my wife, Rachel, had in breaking a few fingers. We were walking our dogs one evening not long after sundown. It was a warm, late-spring dusk in Los Angeles, so we weren't expecting any of the midsummer mischief that typically occurs in our neighborhood each year around that time.

Nevertheless, as we were strolling along the sidewalk a sudden fireworks set the night sky thunderingly ablaze. Our dogs at once panicked and began lunging hard ahead, desperate to get back home. In that moment, Rachel hit a break in the concrete and, leash still in hand, she slowly, almost balletically went down. The pull of the dog continued her roll over her own fingers, and when she lifted her hand into the fire-seared light they bent at angles oddly askew. Three of her fingers crooked upwards, yet they were also cocked backwards, all witchy and malformed. The hand seemed something out of some cinematic horror, and at her command I pulled them straight.

She said the pain was the worst she'd ever experienced, but thinking them only dislocated, we managed our way back home, bandaged up the hand, had a tea and tried to put right in our conversation what had gone terribly wrong – the requisite what ifs and what should've beens.

Throughout the night and into the morning, Rachel said she practiced seeing the pain not as an occurrence in her physical body but as an appearance in her mind, and whenever she was able to do this the pain became so minimal that it virtually disappeared. When her mind drifted from the practice, such as when it fell into reliving the fall, thinking how it could have been avoided, or damn those fireworks! – the pain immediately returned to excruciating levels. In these moments she would remind herself to return to the practice of seeing the pain in mind, and in doing this the pain would quickly diminish.

She continued in and out of this process even when, the next morning, the doctors were resetting all the fingers, which had each cracked cleanly at the knuckle, so that even when the doctor pulled each finger out of joint to place it back into proper alignment, she watched it all occur in mind as opposed to experiencing it directly through the body, and all along she said the pain, though clearly present, was quite manageable. Interestingly, she had only been meditating for one year, and only doing mind recognition training for a few months, yet still she found the technique to be incredibly effective.

Ultimately, we are to use this same practice at the approach of death, and upon death's arrival we continue our practice of resting in innate mind, of seeing the body within the expanse of our own empty awareness. In doing this, we do not experience death as a grueling, pain-pervading experience occurring in the body. Rather, we observe the dissolution of our form within the space of an open, wholly tranquil mind, a mind we see will continue on even in the body's departing.

If we've been practicing in this way prior to the arrival of dying, then what we see at the end of this life is not an ending at all. Rather, it is more of a shedding, or a "shuffle[ing] off" of what Shakespeare calls our "mortal coil." We see, within our awareness, the coil shuffle off as mere observance, not as a loss, just as one might nonchalantly observe a snake shedding off its dead skin at its time of molting. The snake sheds its skin without any sense of loss, nor does it have any attachment to what's being left behind.

This is exactly the experience when seeing the body's release from the perspective of realized awareness. From the point of view of conceptual mind, however, the experience is more highly charged. It can be overwhelming, entirely traumatic, even terrifying. Yet for a practitioner who has trained in realizing emptiness, the experience of releasing the body at the time of dying can be entirely peaceful, and also quite beautiful.

From the perspective of lucid observation, death is not an adversary but yet another empty concept, one we've been able to shed in coming to know our natural state. In observing death's approach through trained awareness, we do not experience the potential trauma of it, because death isn't being perceived conceptually. As a result, fear, pain, anger, sadness never arrive in our experience since the experience is not of an ending but one with a timeless ongoing.

As it pertains specifically to the body, we see in awareness that its falling away will shortly give rise to another body in this same awareness, much as a bird dips out of an open sky, momentarily lost from view, then rises back into that same sky on its continued journey through flight. The bird being our body as it dips away in death, takes flight in another body in the same sky of awareness. We see, as our actual view, this wide-open sky of unbroken awareness upon the body's failing, and we see as well that just because our body falls from flight, the sky of awareness does not disappear. Rather, awareness remains and is always in view.

Dzogchen practice leads us directly to this view in life and, importantly, when death turns its ineliminable eye in our direction. That day is surely coming, and we'll want to meet death's gaze with our fearless own, which sees not a dying but the measureless sky of our eternal flight. Death, in this state of awakened mind, becomes a beautiful departure from the planetary bodies – our own as well as this beautiful Earth we find ourselves on, which throughout our time here has so wonderfully cared for us. Even in dying the energies of Earth are supporting our transition through consciousness, be it into awakening or into another body.

In life, however, we must continue to look at all that keeps us fixed, and all that diminishes us as conscious, creative beings. We start with considering our labels, and we continue to shed from there. As labels are considered, then accordingly released, associated thoughts, behaviors, actions, habitual reactions are let go of as well. This is incredibly beneficial, and it is also entirely liberating. We are alive and awakening, and through this practice we learn to see, then experientially know, how our own innate mind cannot be classified nor ever contained by the reductive, constrictive designations we place on ourselves.

In observing mind in its natural state, and resting there, we see through direct perception that these labels do not belong, but more importantly we see there is nowhere for such designations to attach, since our presence in awareness disallows for such couplings.

In maintaining presence, and in looking at these concepts through lucid perception, we create something else that is critically important: a new perspective, yes, but also new habits. In returning to the addiction label and the impulses and behaviors which give rise to that one label, a new habit is created when we regularly look at impulses in their emergence, or look at the behaviors as they initiate themselves into action. The very act of this observance – of being mindful in the moment – mutes the impulse and countermands impulsive action, and this inches us toward control.

The practice also provides for the additional element of time, and for anyone who sees themself as being an addict, time is an all-essential space to open into. Time allows us to consider, rather than to unconsciously or habitually act. It puts us in the more empowering space of being the objective, non-connected observer, where we are able to take precious seconds to see the actual distinctions of our desire: from where in the body do they arise, what do they look like, do they have a shape, a personality, a coded language that speaks to us or through us?

You observe a craving as if it were an actual entity, and if it's been with you for quite some time then you can even speak to it as if it were an old friend, one whom, yes, has gotten you into some trouble, but there have been good times along the way as well, have there not? To this latter point, it's important not to see this so-called addiction as an enemy in need of banishment. Instead, it is a presence you are attempting to understand, one you are wanting to know just a little better, much as you'd want to more intimately know any of the partners you allow to enter your life.

The practice has you laying your mind's eye directly on the craving in the higher quest of knowing, of understanding, and you're looking to see what, exactly, the impulse is about. There'll be not much in the finding, and that is the point. The one act of looking, then, both empowers the observer and diminishes the desire in one fell swoop.

In terms of time, this is all taking place in very short intervals, being that the technique is employed in those moments when the desire is calling on you to act. Whenever it does, you move again and again into observance mode until the intensity of the cravings begins to wane, for in the unyielding glare of our analytical gaze there is none that won't wither under the lamp of awareness.

More importantly than time, however, is the distance this exercise creates whenever you turn the inner eye on that which arises in the psychic body, in that the entity you seek falls further and further away on each occasion you lay your awareness on it.

We must let go of our labels, all of them, because, first, they are false, but then they're also not particularly helpful, especially if the pursuit is a spiritual one. To that end, the designations we place on ourselves dependably slow us down, even hobble us to the point where we can never properly walk the path. Our shackles are cognitive, and each time we tether ourselves to any signpost of self, calling ourselves this or saying we are that, we self-impose a handicap. "I am a spiritual person." "I am a Buddhist." You may practice Buddhism and adhere to its tenets, but you are not *inherently* Buddhist. Seek the source of that label and you'll surely find there is no Buddhist in the actual body. Nor can this nebulous idea of being spiritual be found anywhere within, either.

Consciously detach from your own self-sanctioning titles and the spiritual high-ground you seek will unfold in ways you might never have imagined. This, because the windows into those higher terrains are newly open, free from the sooted panes that once glassed you off. No longer, after laying bare and lifting away your old labels, will you ever again see through any one fixed lens. Neither addict nor spiritual seeker, you need only be an openness, a gentle presence in awareness, for wisdoms from every direction to arrive, though such wisdoms will always arise most prominently from within. Identity, that is to say, stands in the way of our own wise arrival in that it fills the openness with objects of self, our presence stuck-through with entitling flags.

This word 'identity' is a frank one, for it literally tells us to ID [the] entity. And while its meaning is overtly denoted, it is also an emphatic instruction. We're often saying to ourselves, but also to others, "I am [this]" in reference to one of our many identities. The word in alacritous response says, "alright, please ID [this] entity." Here, the entity which we ID is nothing other than that which we call our nominal self. Entity number one is the 'I.' Building on the foundation of that ground-level entity is the rest of the countless designations we attach to that 'I' – "I am a man;" "I am a writer;" "I'm a teacher;" "I'm an activist."

"I am an addict," and the question we are looking at here in this one practice is: are you *inherently* an addict? The answer is definitively *no* because no addict can be found in the very body bearing the designation. Yes, you might often find yourself in modes of addiction, and these modes might be ongoing for shorter or longer periods of time, but the modes themselves do not initiate any actual transmutation into addict. The same holds true for depression or whatever the condition you see yourself suffering through, for such conditions are always periodic and never absolute. They do not and cannot define in the inherent sense.

The realization of this is a personal one, and it is not meant to be turned into philosophical fuel against your accusers or as some new identity in the opposite, as in "I am *not* an addict." The point here is to release any kind of designation one way or the other, for neither work to your benefit, particularly if your goal is to realize the true nature of your own mind, which point-in-fact is nothing other than an empty awareness absent of any identity. So if you're thinking you can align with your own natural state through any of your identities, you'll not be successful. The natural state can only be realized by releasing all such concepts of front-and-center self.

Admittedly, this can be a very dry exercise, this looking at not only the binding labels but where in ourselves they actually land, where they stick. And like anything that is dry, the knowing that comes in the finding is initially short-lived, in part because this knowing lacks the adhering nectars that typically come with experience. Acknowledgments arrive in awareness like particulates buoyant in the air, which we are able to see but not fully seize before floating further downwind.

Tsoknyi Rinpoche speaks to this initial knowing as lacking *moisture*, because it enters our experience first as a concept. In other words, we mentally see there is no addict found in the physical body, we can acknowledge it, yet the initial seeing is not a full-bodied knowing because what's lacking are the 'moistures' that come from experience in this knowing. With time, such moistures do come. Yet they come immediately when our practice takes us straight into recognizing our own mind in its natural state. In this state, we see and profoundly experience a self absent of any addict, a clear and irrefutable absence that before recognizing may have had us wholly in its hold, this idea of *being* an addict.

But even without recognizing innate mind, there are other elements we can bring into our practice that would help to release and therein deepen our experience in knowing our truer state, and these would be such things as cultivating the more enlightened qualities of compassion, love, devotion to a higher source, joy in one's own being and a developed trust in one's own considered perspective – all of these being the necessary qualities that add moisture to our experience of knowing.

Now, this idea of 'moisture' is neither positive nor negative, which means it can be either positive or negative, depending on how these things play out. In the neutral sense, 'moisture' can be seen as something that substantiates, gives content and proportion to; it imbues. Calling oneself anything, though particularly if there is a potential stigma embedded in the designation, can contain all of the stigma's inherent moistures which likely will not be conducive to one's efforts at realizing the essence of innate mind, for those moistures create frontal perceptions that are incredibly hard to move beyond, or see through. Shame, guilt, sadness, a sense of worthlessness, or even a righteous arrogance, all of these deepen the experience and enliven it as well, so that the experience embodies itself *within the concept*, wherein perception becomes all the more clouded by concept. This further incarnates the 'I' and gives it its own special sauce.

Considering oneself an addict doesn't necessarily mean any of those embodying moistures are implicit, but for many newly aligning with the idea that they are seen as an addict, and must now embrace the designation of 'addict' lest they are seen as being in denial, well, this seemingly slight imposition can be considered one such experiential moisture. Other moistures are further infused into the adhering designation when, as part of the 'treatment,' the designated addict must stand up and say aloud to the group, "I am an alcoholic" or "I am a drug addict," wherein the possible experience of shame or guilt, particularly if there is a knowing of deeds misdone, can be a powerful binding element of one's identity to the designation, so that both self and designation come together as an indistinguishable one.

Merely recognizing through analysis that no actual addict exists in the body at first lacks the binding moistures Tsoknyi Rinpoche speaks to, so we must cultivate them. How do we do this? How do we deepen our knowing of the *non*-concept – not the *counter* concept of "I am *not* an addict," but the absence of any concept of whether you are an addict or not – how do we release the concept altogether?

There are several things we can do to deepen in oneness with a self no longer bound by concepts, by designations whose singular design is to classify and define, and this comes ironically by fully embracing the nominal self we aim to release.

In terms of exercises, the first of these is largely symbolic, but since symbols are incredibly powerful it is good to embrace the act as symbol, as ritual. It begins with simply writing down on a piece of paper the concept you'd like to release. If it is 'addict,' then write "I am an addict." And then you set up a discreet, fire-safe area somewhere outdoors, dig a small hole in the ground, and you take the paper and say whatever you'd like to it – loving, kind words, as if speaking to an old friend before letting them go.

Speak to this old friend, this designation, as a eulogy of sorts, and then with absolute love and gratitude, and with whatever ritual displays you'd like to bring into this one act of letting go, you light the paper afire. You can even say something like, "and with this flame I burn away old concepts of myself. I free myself from all concepts of who I am. I am confidently and lovingly letting go of this old identity of being an addict," or something to that effect. And then you drop the burning designation into the hole dug in the earth and ceremonially bury it after seeing it totally burn. Bury it, soil and ash, with the intention that the earth itself will bring renewal, both to the idea that transmuted in fire and the designation that arose as smoke to the sanctioning gods.

Be aware that it is you as well who is sanctioning the arrival of a more open, less compromised self, one who carries one less concept about who you claim yourself to be. If you are able, you can sit there in quiet contemplation, and with a loving, wholly open heart, consider the person you've just let go of and offer that person love and safe tidings on their journey into new and renewing, wholly cleansing realms.

The other thing you can do is again write, but this time it is an epistolary activity in which you write a letter to the person you've just let go of. This was 'you' only moments before. It is not you now because you've considerately released that one individual. You are writing to the 'you' who till moments before had so dutifully, even nobly walked with the designation 'addict.' What strength this took, and what upright character it truly exhibited.

You write a letter to this 'old you,' if you want to call it that, and say whatever it is you need to say. These things are quite personal, but if you're looking for guidelines then perhaps you can speak to why this 'old you' had been deemed an addict in the first place. You can acknowledge the span of time this honorable individual carried the waving flag of that one label, and how the time has come to release that designation, that defining concept, in order to grow into the more liberated and enlightened self that awaits – the more expansive being who one day wishes to awaken into the light of full consciousness, an enlightened awareness that by nature has no defining or limiting modes. There is so much to say, and take the time to say it all. Be as detailed and forthright as need be. Be loving, understanding, compassionate, supportive, be totally honest and unconditionally forgiving. Be committed to a new way of seeing and being, a new way of acting toward yourself and others, and these ideas, too, get written as well.

What is to be done with this letter? Well, you can either hold onto it, place it away somewhere where only you have access to it – if, that is, you ever want to read it again. More powerfully, however, because again it taps into ritual, is to burn the letter in the same way you burned the defining designation. You offer high sentiments as smoke to the gods, and you lay this old self into the rebirthing earth, remembering in the act that this rebirthing is your own.

The last thing we can do after both of these rituals, but it can be done anytime afterwards – it does not need to happen on the spot – is to sit in quiet consideration of yourself. At some point in this consideration, envision you 'the addict,' who was just symbolically released, side by side with you now, who no longer carries the weight of that onetime designation. You both are the same person, but one bears the weight of what is now old, while the other, the current you, has let that weight go.

Imagine a child who feels they've done something terribly wrong – perhaps they've accidentally killed a bird with the slingshot they just received as a birthday gift, and they come to you heartbroken and heavy. Your instincts tell you to pull the child in, to embrace this lovely soul with all the understanding and compassion you can offer, and you lift them warmheartedly in their unbearable experience of loss.

Now, an addict may or may not overtly feel this same weight of sorrow beneath the designation they bear, but what drives the addict to drink or do drugs or seek any number of the destructive behaviors they are accused of and perhaps even hold themselves responsible for, well, the totality of this can be quite heavy indeed. It is all of that which, in letting go of the label, we must forgive ourselves for before the label can be fully and forever released. Forgiveness is key. We must allow ourselves to forgive.

And so you envision the old you, the addict you, next to you now, and you see in this vision a heartfelt forgiving of the addict for all that had led to the arrival of the designation: the behaviors exhibited while in the full throws of the drug, but also the pain and confusion which led to those behaviors in the first place, a lifetime of experiences that spoke to drugs as being the preferred mode of existing, for this path seemingly delivered the least amount of pain. Perhaps, even for a short while, there was shame in the very act of accepting that label, "I, Addict," acknowledging the weight of that designation and all the days you since walked with it. This is a profound exchange of love and forgiveness from one very real aspect of yourself to another.

Again, it's important to bring up the idea that this is not a banishment of the other. You are not banishing anyone. You are, rather, envisioning and then expressing your genuine love, as well as offering your most sincere forgiveness to *yourself*, your higher self embracing the self who had suffered so dearly and learned to attend to that suffering by reaching for a drink or drugs or whatever it was, if only to soften the pain.

The other thing here you should never forget is this: an addiction is nothing other than a misguided pursuit toward wholeness, toward a sense of feeling complete, of lacking nothing. We sedate because we suffer, and suffering is the cyclonically propelling force for transformative practice, and towards transformation.

We largely live in cultures that provide little in the way of higher spiritual trainings, ones that would empower us with the utilizing tools for healing ourselves on all levels, tools we could employ upon immediate need without having to wait days or even weeks to see an 'official' clinician or sanctioned practitioner, then years before seeing any results even from that. Without those tools, we turn to drink or drugs or sexual gratification or an entire gamut of behaviors that can easily lead to addiction, if only to find peace within. Yet the only way to find true inner peace is in directly seeing, then coming to know oneself through inward sight.

We need come into alignment with our own higher purpose – why are we here? – and the highest of those purposes is to recognize our own inner nature, our naturally pure state which is the core of ourselves. It is who we truly are as timeless, ageless, undying beings, and it is right here within, easily accessible and ready to engage with. This natural state is totally open, wholly awakened and is entirely one with the fullness of our universe and with all in existence. It is, in other words, the supreme source of our highest self, of who we aim to be, and we need only recognize it and ultimately align with it to arrive there.

In the moment of recognizing our mind's natural state, we see irrefutably there is no addict, but we also see there is nothing else, either. What is present instead is only potential: to be anything, even an addict, but more beautifully and magnificently to be an enlightened presence on this planet, one where such labels lift to the winds, rise and die away into the transformative rays of our own symbolic suns.

The Ground

Awareness is self-luminous and is one with space. Seeing space, one sees the container for awareness, hence the container for the entirety and full complexity of our self. As you perceive, you do so only through space, from the emptiness of it, for the perceiving mind is of this same emptiness. And while awareness, for now, is rooted in the body, it nonetheless never leaves the boundless, sourceless space which gives rise to that which we see as the body of ourself.

The body, you'll recall, is a near totality of space. Awareness is present throughout all of it. In this way, that which we call the body exists only in our awareness, not the other way around. As you sit in meditation, the ache in your foot, as much as the conceptual mind would like to tell you is happening in the foot, is actually occurring only in your awareness. You are aware of it. If you weren't aware of it, there would be no ache. The throb in the foot here, the evening amber of light there, the dog dreaming, heavily breathing over there, the crickets out there, the galaxy aglimmer up there: all this occurs in no other place than awareness. It is night now, but the day dawns only in awareness.

We are a body of awareness, and that body, including its seeming sum of flesh, is nothing other than the natural expression of innate mind. Thus it is empty. How is it empty? Space is both point-zero and sum-total of our embodied selves, and we can find nothing of ourselves that cannot be analyzed right back down to the emptiness of space. It is in this very space where we observe the mind, where we see firsthand the oneness of the two. Mind and space are inseparably one.

Mind, the naturally occurring one, sees not so much the dog, not so much the stars, but *itself* in observance of these and all other appearances. Mind sees mind, and within it in great oneness is the appearance of our seated self, the stirless movement of intermittent thought, the setting in which we sit which perhaps permits for the vaulting view of the firmament above and the universe in its infinince beyond, all of which can only be found in the space of our awareness.

How does one arrive here, at this eminence in sight? You first recognize a mind that has no origin, location, no destination or cessation, and in this recognition you simply rest. You sit with it and observe, remaining mindful yet relaxed. In the stillness, all obscurations begin to naturally disappear, wherein the muddiness of mundane mind gives way to the clarity of its natural state. Awareness settles into the openness of itself, is at ease in that openness, in perfect balance, empty of all concepts, in allowance of all that appears.

It is often said, perhaps to the point of cliché, that appearances in mind – thoughts, things, places and people – are like reflections in a mirror. We plainly see, without any confusion, that appearances in the mirror are empty in that we recognize them for what they are: mere reflections. We also know, again without confusion, that whatever appears in the mirror is not other than the mirror, not separate from it, but wholly one within it. Say, for instance, the mirror catches in its frame a window, and outside that window is the glorious rising of the moon, all blood in its autumnal ruddiness. An owl in crimson rays sits lightly on a limb, its molten eyes in mirror of the night. The framing of the window, the fullness of the moon, the owl in lunar light: these in the mirror are not a multiplicity but of a oneness within. They are not seen as, nor would they be mistaken for yet another moon, yet another bird, yet another branch. As appearance they arise in oneness, of an essence that is singular and inseparable from the mirror's glass. Because of this they are said to be of one taste, and they are seen to be just that.

We see this same oneness when resting in the natural state. We see ourselves amongst all else as a oneness within. All is of one taste. All in the openness is observed as emptiness since all that appears is of a single essence, the pure articulation of intrinsic awareness.

Awareness in this way finds parallel with the mirror.

The reflections we see in a mirror, reflections of form, are analogous, in terms of emptiness, to these same appearances we observe in mind. Whether observing the form of ourselves or the myriad forms perceived as other, from the perspective of the natural state it is all seen as bare appearance, thus none other than emptiness.

Our perception of emptiness, then, is unambiguously clear in as much as its essence is utterly seen, therein it is known.

Across the Tropics

As sentient, seeking beings, depending on the lifetime, we are either on an unshakeable quest toward inward knowing or, oppositely, we find ourselves fully engaged with the world we are currently in. At cyclical points in our ongoing existence, each of us enter the arc toward 'spirit,' toward wanting to awaken, and this can last an entire life or several lifetimes before once again we inevitably cycle out of that inward quest to know.

What is it we desire to know? What is it we so insatiably seek, spend lifetimes striving to expose? It is that which is eternally within us, our baseline selves we need only see, recognize, then ultimately realize.

These arcs – the risings and fallings of 'feeling spiritual,' of questing for the higher self – are part of even larger cycles which themselves coincide with larger and smaller arcs of energies and their infinite expressions. The arc of this day's anger or depression perhaps bends perfectly under the arc of the week's anger or depression, which itself is but a mode of some longer arc which somehow textures the life and loosely defines its general trajectory. Along the shorter arcs there are good hours and good days, but sure enough the moment arrives when we encounter our own inner fire, which so often seems sparked by events from without; or we sense the weighty shadow gathering within and know a fall toward some fathomless darkness is near upon.

We know these shorter cycles. We all experience them to one degree or another. But it is important to be aware of the longer cycles these bouts fall under, and to acknowledge at their start that, as with everything else, these cycles inevitably come to an end before new cycles of differing energies shape themselves into recognizable patterns.

We can engender new cycles by consciously, and with the highest of intention, bringing old cycles to a close. The cycle of the addict is a good example of this active closure which had as its guiding lantern the sincere and heartfelt desire to create something new, something lighter and more uplifting, more life affirming.

That said, cycles on their own will both come into being and come to an end when we take no action at all – that is, when we bring no awareness to their beginnings or endings. Without awareness, we suffer through the requisite highs and lows of our various cycles, however large or small those cycles might be. The smaller cycles, relatively speaking, which involve anger, depression, even states of prolonged happiness, can go on for years or even decades until they naturally die out or we consciously reduce the charge so their energies no longer trigger unwanted behaviors.

Cycles, too, can end in death, but they can also quite naturally end mid-life, where we then look back on what seemed like another life or an entirely different person prior to 'the crisis' (how interesting, our use of this word, 'crisis,' in referencing our midlife change). Typically, upon entering this midlife change, there is often excitement accompanied with a sense of joyous liberation at what might lie ahead. Whatever that may be, the experience, at least in the short run, is likely to be enlivened by energies freshly charged and by a mind more open, more accepting than this same mind mere months before. It could be a new love, a new job, a new and radically altered perspective on the world. Any and all of these can be both indication and affirmation of a new cycle on the rise. But be conscious of the fact that the new love or new job might be one in the same with the last, and here again you are being asked to either wake up to the longer cycle, to see it for what it actually might be, or continue to live unconsciously through its predictable highs and lows, its fleeting moments of joy and familiar periods of suffering.

The arc of this lifetime did not begin at birth. That seeming beginning is a false marker in consciousness, for in seeing birth from the perspective of awareness, we see ourselves passing through a layer of consciousness, so to speak, much in the way sleep gives way to our waking state. The 'layer' we experience as being our birth is really a transiting between states of consciousness. Prior to entering the womb, our doorway into this life, the mind wanders in a state of consciousness known as 'the karmic bardo of becoming.' This bardo 'in-between,' which often is loosely referred to as the bardo of death, is the state of consciousness we experience between bodies, and our way of perceiving here is similar to the way we perceive in dream – itself known as 'the bardo of dream.' The karmic bardo of becoming, simply put, is a state of consciousness which occurs after having permanently left a physical body, and since it is our own mind in a fluidly transitioning state, this bardo inevitably gives way to the perceiving consciousness of the lifetime we are now in, known as 'the natural bardo of this life.'

These various bardos, and the states of consciousness they align with, are not merely speculative, mere postulations we either choose to believe in or not. They are actual and predictable states of mind, of sentience and experience – as actual and predictable as the dream states we enter upon falling asleep. In sleep, we are either totally unconscious or dreaming, and we cycle between those two states the entire time we are 'not awake.' Then, predictably, we wake up from sleep and find ourselves in the bardo of this life, which again is yet another state of consciousness that is predictable in that, in the conceptual sense, it dependably occurs. We expect to wake up from sleep because we know this is part of the normal cycle of this life. The karmic bardo of becoming transpires with this kind of predictability. In other words, *it will occur,* just as surely as the bardo of this life occurs after you transit out of the bardo of dream. And on and on the cycles continue, ad infinitum, until our meditation practice one day pulls us from these deluded states and delivers us into the awakened, unchanging state we call 'the natural state,' or what is more poetically referred to as wisdom mind, enlightened mind, buddha mind. That is to say, these differing bardo states, all conceptual, dissolve the moment we enter mind in its natural state.

Our longer arcs of energy, then, cross through all the bardos as part of a continuum, for they are energies wholly integrated with conceptual mind. You might notice, for instance, that your state of mind during the day to some degree manifests in the dreams you experience through night. Then in the morning, these same energies remain present in the form of a lingering, a residue, a spillover of a sort. Note the two bardos those energies moved through. This occurs at every scale and across the various bardos.

If you were midway through your energy arc at birth, then it is likely the same situations will arise in the early part of this life as when you left the last. If this is so, then you may experience in this lifetime the ending of that arc sometime 'midlife.' As it cycles to its natural close, it heads toward the zero-point. If we equate this to a sine wave, this zero-point would be the midline in the sinusoidal graph.

See yourself, energy-wise, as an ongoing sine wave with a midline running straight through the center of your eternal being. This midline, the equator of your ongoing conceptual self, has no beginning and no end and so is beyond birth and dying. It is along this midline where we find the longer periods of peace and ease in our lives, because it is along this line we are at our most inward-looking or mindfully being. We are, it can be said, feeling more 'spiritual,' this because we are naturally nearing balance, for we are closing in or hovering near our center, our core selves, where we are most receptive to the call of our natural state.

Above and below this midline we find the tropics, equatorially speaking – the Tropic of Cancer and the Tropic of Capricorn, we could call them. Above those tropic lines we are riding solidly on the prevailing winds of one or several concurrent cycles, including their corresponding micro-cycles – and, remember, these cycles can last through a single lifetime or across several.

Above one of the tropics, as a simplified example, we are experiencing a life of utter good fortune – a CEO of a successful company, a happy marriage and many beautiful friends, though not to imply this good fortune isn't without its trials and trying times. Every life has its suffering – suffering being the first of the four noble truths. But some lives are notably low on the scale of suffering while others seem entirely steeped in it.

Above the other latitudinal tropic, we might be experiencing lives that are relentlessly challenging, with ill fortune seemingly around every turn. Neither of these lives are good or bad, per se. They merely are what they are: predictable, perhaps even mappable experiences upon the trades of conceptual mind.

On the downward trajectory of either of those arcs, dropping below the tropic lines, we cross into the subtropic latitudes and move auspiciously toward the equatorial zones. At the midline we reach the equator, which could be equated to either a mind totally at ease or, if one has been training, a mind which has realized 'no mind.'

It is between these two latitudinal lines, Cancer and Capricorn, where we are most in the mind of being or feeling spiritual, since we are either arcing toward or away from the equator. In whichever direction this arc leads us, as long as we are in the subtropics we are still 'in the zone,' still within the region of awakening energies which tend toward equilibrium, as opposed to variance or imbalance.

It is in this large geographical zone, the subtropics of ourselves, where our potential for recognizing no mind is greatest. If you are reading this book, or if you have spent a lifetime searching for the truth of who you are, it is likely you are somewhere in the subtropics of that ever-arcing self. Recognizing 'no mind,' or that which we call our natural mind, will bring you into the unvarying zone of equatorial awareness, our awakened state.

If we are unable to recognize wisdom mind during this most opportune period, we slip past the equator or move higher through the subtropics, where we then continue into the next cycle of lifetimes: the new arc of conceptual experience.

On both sides of the equatorial midline, which is a fairly large geographical landscape of experience, there is opportunity to enlighten, to realize our highest consciousness, because we are being pulled somewhat magnetically toward the center of our being. It is a kind of gravitational pull toward our more authentic self, the fully realized self in that our awareness within is already awakened, primordially pure, for this is its natural state. The 'center of our being' is in fact absent of self, for in recognizing and then stabilizing in no mind, no self can possibly exist, nor is one even faintly experienced. This is the awakening we did not know we sought until we arrived here, for our awakening is into an emptiness where the only 'other' is awareness, which in truth cannot be intellectually understood; it can only be experienced.

If you are feeling the pull toward so-called spirit, if you have embraced spiritual practice and embarked on a life of attempting to do right by yourself and by the high principles of a loving community, not to mention the full-throated demands of the earth we live on, then it is likely you are now in the subtropics of your own cyclical experience, either aiming toward or drifting away from the equator of your truer self. The importance of this critical positioning should not be ignored, for it means you are most ready, and most able, to recognize your own natural state. Take the time in this lifetime to do just that, for the opportunity this state of mind brings is indeed a rare one and the moment, should you miss it, will surely pass.

Note again that the midline of the sinusoid, which we can equate to the equatorial line of our eternal selves, is stable and ongoing. It doesn't change. Of course, this is only a graphic indication of the idea that in realizing no mind, we from that point forward experience an awareness that is stable, unchanging and ever ongoing, what the Buddhist call buddha mind or our own buddha nature.

Many of us have experienced this buddha mind, even if we didn't recognize it at the time. It arrives in our awareness every now and again, though without someone pointing it out to us we are unable to see it for what it is, which is why learning how to recognize is so essential to our awakening. There is a flash experience of this natural state at the point of orgasm. There is a moment in each of our deaths where we experience and are in profound witness of our own buddha nature, and it is at this moment in particular when we have the greatest opportunity to awaken, though only if we've been preparing through training in this lifetime. There is, interestingly, the point of contact in a terrible accident where we experience mind in its natural state: it is the moment where the fourth time opens before us, where present time seemingly stops and our experience of the instant is of absolute clarity, peace, stillness, a wholly objective awareness even in the midst of the full-blown chaos and catastrophe of, say, a car crash. Others have experienced their own buddha nature while running a long-distance marathon, or swimming. In meditation we often cross into the natural state, yet without the teachings, without someone pointing this mind out to us, we do not recognize it.

In not recognizing, we lose an opportunity to truly know the essence of ourselves, which is empty. In recognizing this natural mind when we experience it, we see this emptiness. We see there is no self, that the body is likewise a no-thing in the space of our awareness, a mere appearance. We see, in this same state, that our identities are also nothing more than concepts, thus they are empty. We see that appearances, too, are of this same emptiness, of the kind we see in dream. In seeing this in the awakened space of no mind, it truly is an eye-opening realization. It is not the full awakening we speak to which arrives through ongoing practice and ultimate realization, but it is an awakening nevertheless.

Without recognizing our own innate nature in those rare moments we've been able to experience it, we still experience the bliss, clarity and fully lucidity of that short-lived moment, but we do not importantly recognize the essence of that awareness, and so critical insight is not developed, a moment of reflective pause does not take root, and the cycles of conceptual thinking continue until the day comes when we are fortunate enough to receive mind recognition teachings in the formal sense.

Perhaps this is your moment of fortunate reception; perhaps it is just a passing through. Either way is as it should be, for the moment of our awakening can only arrive when we are ready to open our eyes. Like rousing from a fitful slumber, sometimes it takes a minute to see ourselves into the light, and sometimes we want only to tuck ourselves deeper into dream and remain there just a bit longer.

The Journey

We are conscious beings in carnate form. It cannot be said we don't exist because we experience. Our experience points to an existence. Yet how is it we exist, and who is it that experiences? We find under analysis neither an 'I' nor a body. The body, it turns out, is a grand sum of emptiness, reducible in every way to the level of space. In finding no body, we naturally find no existence of an 'I.' Both, as seen through direct perception, are but empty concepts, complex constructions of conceptual mind.

What, then, experiences? Only our awareness experiences. Without awareness the body would be a corpse. A corpse cannot hear. A corpse cannot see. A corpse cannot smell. It does not taste. It no longer feels. It cannot name itself nor tell a single story about itself. Only a mind can do these things. When a mind leaves the body there is no one left. The corpse at one time identified with a self. It had an 'I.' That 'I' departed with the mind, and what remains is a body no more. We now call it 'corpse.'

With a mind, the body experiences. It is for this reason we look at mind as being the source of our existence, for all that we know and experience. How do we know we exist? Because we perceive, which is another way of saying we know. What is it that perceives? Only our awareness perceives. It doesn't matter whether awareness is in conceptual mode or is knowing non-conceptually, it still perceives. A corpse cannot do this.

We meditate because we know a corpse awaits the body of our experience, and we want to know what happens next. What happens next is already present in our own minds, and we need only recognize the nature of this mind to know the answer to all. In recognizing our own innate nature, we see nothing more needs to be done. This is the singular practice, and it is one which takes us to the source of our very selves, the ground-level being of all existence.

Recognize your own mind, get to know it, and your search for anything beyond, or anything other, will come to an immediate end, for in that recognition you'll see there is no other and there is no beyond. It is all right here, as it always has been.

The mind we aim to recognize is the source of love, joy, and compassion, three qualities we associate with all enlightened beings. When we rest in mind's essence, and do this often through daily practice, those three qualities begin to imbue our every aspect. They permeate throughout the total of ourselves, through our every expression. These qualities fill the space of our body in such ways that allow for little else to enter – not illness, but not depression either. Anxiety does not enter, and nor will fear or even anger, unless the anger is truly righteous, meaning conscious – that human/civil rights kind of anger that demands humans across the planet rise into their best selves.

Practicing every day, inhabiting presence each day, recognizing that which is our essence and resting in this extraordinary space again and again can allow for love, joy, and compassion to be the sum of our expression, all in the short course of this one lifetime. That is to say, we can awaken in this lifetime. It might not be a full awakening into enlightened being in this one lifetime, though that too is possible. But even the lesser awakenings, the smaller day to day ones we experience in our practice, allow us to become so much more infused with all the qualities we could ever wish for, for it was all we ever sought.

The teachings in *Entering the Mind* can be practiced starting today. There is no need to wait for the perfect teacher to arrive in your life and transmit them to you. Seek the master and the master will come, and right now the master is you. That master, which is nothing short of your own innate mind, is within the hermetic cave of your own enlightened being, and the master awaits your presence. This demands a turning in.

If you are looking for your purpose in this life, then there is no higher purpose than to embody your own internal master, the guru of awakened self who calls for your attendance. That master, you'll recall, is as close to you as your finger is to space. Look at your finger now. How far must it move to touch the space it is already in? Your own high master is this close.

Recognize your own essence and the arrival is upon.

In doing this by yourself, the biggest obstacle you'll encounter, it should be emphatically noted, is your own story, so check this story going into each and every practice. Are you really what you say you are? Be willing to shed any and every story that has you in relation to something else, has you circling like a vulture to readily pick at the carcass of past events, or sees you sailing dove-like into futures existent only in imagination. These futures do not and will not ever exist in the real because the very instant a moment changes the imagination changes, therein the story changes and with it any wondered time to come. Our stories, then, hinder our progress in the present here-and-now, in part because they sap all energy from such progress, not to mention they distract.

Let your stories go and a familiar looseness will come in return, the same looseness that was in you as a child when stories told of you, and by you, were few. Another important point to make here is that when our stories are allowed to fall, we can read even words on a page and quiet, transformational truths come into reveal, this because our own tale does not get in the way.

Refer again to the fable of the pilgrimage which first began this telling. The questions there, imparted from the lips of an enlightened sage, are the very questions you would ask yourself when entering the mind you seek to recognize. These simple questions point to what cannot be seen, yet that which cannot be seen can, by your awareness, be plainly known.

Then take yourself further into the tale, to the Ouroboros and the self-swallowing of a perceived self. In meditation, again recognize the mind the sage pointed out to you, and while resting in this recognition seek the knower of that recognition – who is doing the knowing, the recognizing? Who or what is the observer that observes? Seeking this, and becoming aware of awareness seeing itself, is the very self-opening window through which enlightened mind comes into view.

Continue to read the masters, even if you are unable to receive direct teachings from them. And then while practicing, and without your own story getting in the way, try to absorb the subtle truths that might arise from one word here or another word there. Let the words themselves be like light, snowy flakes falling from wintry skies into the warming waters of natural mind, and perhaps one or two will on their own impart some truth which even the wordsman himself had not intended. Things take on a life of their own even after they've been brought into creative being, and words on the page enliven in ways no author could predict, for they land in the heart of a reader in such ways as to breathe new word into the original word.

Forward yourself further in this tale and onward to the 'I,' and find its entity nonexistent, not in any aspect of the physical body, not in any of its parts nor anywhere in the whole. This kind of inquiry can be done only by you, and though it is wise to get instruction directly from a master, you also shouldn't turn away from knowledge being received from other sources, a book for instance, a near death experience, giving birth or any number of other ways we suddenly awaken into mind-altering, life-affirming truths. This includes our meditation practice, which is wellspring to our most transformational insights.

Yet, all that said, there is really nothing quite like receiving these truths from the mouths of great teachers, these realized individuals who say specific things to you because in you they see where such wisdoms will land, whereas to another they say other things that will further that one individual's developing practice.

If you're looking for guidance in finding such masters, I can only point you toward what I know are good sources, though I'm sure there are others I am not aware of. Two traditions in particular should be on your radar: search for masters associated with Mahāmudrā and Dzogchen and you'll find yourself at the headwaters for nearly all the philosophical discussions in this book. You can refine your search to the several lineages associated with those two traditions to find more specific or specialized masters who can point you to all the right instructions up and down the philosophical ladder.

Know that the journey toward finding a master whom you'll love is a personal one, so take your time in the search, set your intentions high, and do take pleasure in all the wonderful people you'll meet along the way. To that end, the sangha itself is worthy of our soul's setting out.

Journey well, and blessings.

www.ingramcontent.com/pod-product-compliance
Lightning Source LLC
Chambersburg PA
CBHW032358040426
42451CB00006B/49